CW01663157

Doctor's Guide to Oil of Wild Oregano

101 Uses

Dr. Cass Ingram

KNOWLEDGE HOUSE PUBLISHERS

Knowledge House Publishers

Printed in the United States of America

ISBN: 9781931078474

Disclaimer: This book is not intended as a substitute for medical diagnosis or treatment. Anyone who has a serious disease should consult a physician before initiating any change in treatment or before beginning any new treatment.

To order this or additional Knowledge House books call: (909) 284 5620 or order via the web at: www.knowledgehousepublishers.com

Printed in the United States of America

Contents

Chapter One

Introduction

"Let food be your medicine" is a compelling dictum delineated by not only Thomas Edison but also by numerous others. In ancient times Hippocrates spoke of this. No wonder—he had wild oregano to prove it. It was the Prophet of Islam, Muhammad, may God's peace and blessings be upon him, who also said so, urging his followers to use whole foods and spices as their medicine cabinet, including black seed, wild oregano, vinegar, and raw honey. Now, it is known that all such natural complexes are medicinal, in fact, virtually drug-like in their powers. In medieval times the of note were strictly herbal extracts as well as essential oils. Yet, among these food-like cures wild oregano takes pre-eminence. It is an extremely diverse natural medicine with far more uses and applications than most people realize. For instance, medieval practitioners recommended it for earaches, congestion, lung disorders, and digestive ailments, including dyspepsia.

It was Langam in his *Garden of Health* published in 1633 who described oregano, particularly the distilled oil, as the ideal therapy for a wide range of conditions, including bladder/urinary disorders, kidney disease, earache, headache, itchy skin, hives, cough, canker sores, oral inflammation, constipation, spastic colon, or intestinal worms, and breast inflammation. He even mentioned it as a treatment for congestive heart failure, a use popularized in ancient Babylon.

Yet can entire book be written just about wild oregano. Is it really that stupendous as a natural remedy? Furthermore, what is oil of wild oregano? Moreover, incredibly, does it and/or its associated supplements actually have 101-plus uses? How could any natural complex possess such an immense degree of utility? Moreover, who would actually realize that the pizza spice has this degree of extensive value as a medicine for human disease?

Oil of wild oregano is a potent concentrate derived, ideally, from 100% wild-growing oregano spice. It is extracted through steam distillation and then emulsified in the appropriate amount of oil, in this case, extra virgin olive oil.

Until the sources described in this book made it known, for instance, the original book on oregano therapy, *The Cure is in the Cupboard*, virtually no one in North America even knew a single therapeutic use for wild oregano and certainly had no clue that its extract, oil of wild oregano, is a potent natural medicine with a multiplicity of uses. Yet, even today, despite increased availability and much scientific substantiation little is known about it. Popularly, it is taken for colds and flu, perhaps bronchitis and pneumonia. Traditionally, it is applied to wounds to prevent infection and also serious injuries, like burns and fractures, to speed healing. The oil is also consumed to bolster the immune system. These are the typical claims that are made, the most common one being that it "fights colds and flu." While this is true, it hardly represents the real and ultimate nature of this novel complex. Nor does it define its extensive historical use. Nor does it quantify its value based on modern science. Here, the full gamut of the benefits of oil of wild oregano will be described. In this regard the complete information will be represented, that is how the individual will gain the greatest degree of benefit from the oil and associated supplements.

The type of oil used makes a difference. The premium type is made from 100% wild-growing oregano, which naturally thrives on high in the Mediterranean mountains. In this regard there is great confusion, much of it disseminated from manufacturers. Oregano oil has become a commodity. Dozens of companies now sell it, though by no means are they the original source. Nor, unlike the original, are these secondary players inventive to any degree with their formulas. Nor do they derive the oregano oil from the original source. Nor do they produce it themselves. Even though it may be bottled and sold by rather large or well- known supplement companies rarely do such companies derive it directly from the wild source.

Regardless, the creation of wild oregano oil is no easy project. It requires the handpicking by skilled, adept villagers of wild-growing oregano in the high mountains, 5000 to 12,000 feet above sea level. It also requires the picking of the correct truly wild—and edible—species. It is the natives who alone are familiar with this. The village people must climb these mountains on foot or via mules. They, then, pick the wild oregano and bring it back to be cool-dried. Subsequently, it is brought to the distillation facility, where it is steam-distilled: without the use of chemicals.

Because it is so arduous, commonly, companies take short-cuts. The number of these short-cuts are legion. As well, most companies are simply unaware of the nature of wild oregano. They merely buy the oil through wholesalers without performing any research and without following the natural and true footprint. For instance, they use wild-type plants but then, grow them in soil. They even clone these plants, corrupting them, to artificially raise the levels of certain active ingredients. These human-altered plants are then grown at lower elevations than the natural ones, like a thousand feet above sea level or even less. Regardless, wild oregano does not grow on soil. Instead, it thrives exclusively on and among rocks: specifically calcareous-rich calcium- phosphate rock. This is what makes it so powerful and also so free of disease. No microbe can survive when exposed to wild, high-mountain oregano.

The essential oil within the plant makes it potent beyond belief with therapeutic powers that are unmatched. In this regard it is important to realize that not all oregano is the same. This is particularly true of the farm-raised type. Typically, oregano grown on soil is fertilized both with chemical and natural fertilizers. Completely in an unnatural environment, because of this it is tainted. It is irrigated, which further corrupts it. Never does this occur in the wild. Moreover, such irrigation causes it to develop mold, a complete bastardization, since oregano is one of the most potent mold-killing substances known.

The farm-raised type is relatively impotent. According to a study conducted by *Economic Botany* it doesn't even produce sufficient oil glands to create the necessary medicinal essential oil. When the underside of the farmed oregano leaves were viewed, the oil glands were missing. Moreover, the profile the of oil it contain is greatly different than that extracted from the true wild species.

Yet another method is simply raising the oregano plants in a completely aberrant environment, like Canada, Europe, and

the United States. Once again, cultivars are selected for artificially high levels of active ingredients, notably carvacrol. The plants are then raised on tilled soil, once again treated with fertilizers and in some cases, herbicides and pesticides. This farm-raised oregano is then distilled, and the resulting oil falsely marketed as either wild or in the case of it being grown organically, as certified organic or USDA organic.

As well, oregano oil is being derived from genetically engineered plants. The primary players here are Israeli and US scientists, who have engineered high carvacrol cultivars. In China as well much oregano oil is being produced. There, too, it never grows naturally. Nor is the climate conducive to producing a truly high-grade of oregano for human use. There are no high-mountain regions consisting of calcium-phosphate rock anywhere in this region, so, once again, it is grown on soil. Regardless, the Chinese type is also cloned to produce high carvacrol oil, as much as 95%, which is an aberration to the extreme. There is no 95% carvacrol found in the Mediterranean-source oregano oil or, in fact, in any oregano oil from anywhere else in the world.

Carvacrol is only one of some 30 different components in a high-grade, whole food wild oregano oil. Though it is important, it is merely a part of a blend of active ingredients that work in a sophisticated synergy. Forcing the plant to produce virtually only this compound does lead to a corruption. This corruption causes the end-product to be unnatural, that is never found in nature. For this reason, it cannot be used on a consistent basis without concern of side-effects and/or toxicity.

There is one company that never does so. It would be ideal to identify this company, as it specializes in wild oregano supplements. However, here, the various wild oregano supplements will be described, generically. Even so, with careful research it is possible to precisely determine the optimal sources of high-grade wild oregano oil. It will also be possible to determine the original brand, which is the most potent, reliable oregano oil complex available.

True wild oregano oil is made from wild-source oregano growing directly on the mountain slopes, which is never artificially produced or farm-raised. Here, it is carefully picked each season by experienced villagers: all by hand, which is itself an impressive feat. Commonly, other oil of oregano supplements are imitations, many of which aren't truly wild or even actual oregano derived. In contrast, the original type, the formula which innovated precisely the idea of the consumption of oregano oil, is wild source, made only from the naturally growing spice found in the high mountains, all the way to the mountain tops.

It is such a pure, true quality. A perennial, the oregano grows in the spring and summer, being harvested towards the end of the season. In the fall it recedes. Then, incredibly, it is covered by snow, still surviving, and re-grows the next year. This is so it can be picked, once again. No one attends to it, other than the wild powers of nature, divinely inspired: the wind, rain, sun, and mountain, rocky matter. There is virtually no soil where oregano thrives, only traces of it mixed among the white, calcium-phosphate rock.

Moreover, everyone knowns the power of calcium- phosphate. This is the complex which makes marble. In fact, versus dirt or soil oregano prefers to grow on marbleized rock and even can be found growing out of the marble ruins of ancient Greek and Roman civilizations.

It can be stated categorically. Though much copied the oil within this bottle is made exclusively from such wild

plants, growing from the peaks of the mountains down to just before the tree level. This is why it is so potent. Moreover, as this is the same as the food spice this explains its value for daily use, that is the fully edible oil of wild oregano. With its robust, spicy taste it is clearly a food supplement of the highest quality and most exceptional efficacy. Other, cheaper oregano oils are not so robust; many may have a bitter, tinny taste, a sign of corruption of the natural chemistry of this complex.

Daily use is crucial, as oil of wild oregano is a significant protective agent. Such regular use prevents the occurrence of virtually any infectious disease, including colds, flu, pneumonia, food poisoning, yeast infections, mold infestation, and infection by drug resistant germs. This type of use also acts to strengthen and enhance the overall immune response, while also preventing a number of other conditions, including food allergy, bronchitis, anaphylaxis, and intestinal disorders.

Other corruptions in oregano oil

There are numerous other corruptions that occur in oregano production and marketing. One of these is the sourcing of the oregano without great care, in this case from high- thymol plants. Thymol has significant toxicity and cannot be consumed in large quantities. This is because it readily causes damage to the heart and liver.

So, what a critical issue it is to define this, so that all people will know the difference, especially in respect to the much needed regular or daily use. It seems so innocuous, as the label does read in most cases "oil of oregano" or "oregano oil," with 'wild' and/or 'organic' also added. People would never think that items labeled as such could be potentially unsafe, particularly if consumed regularly. Yet, this is truly risky if the levels of thymol are excessive. However, this is never the case with the original, true wild oregano oil. With its careful, thorough quality control and guaranteed levels of key active ingredients plus low thymol content, it is this type which can be taken daily, even in large amounts.

In addition, some oregano oils aren't even oregano oil. Instead, they are from entirely different species, including marjoram and thyme, those derived from *Origanum compactum* and *Thymus capitus* being prominent examples. It was Julia Lawless who pointed this out in her book *The Encyclopedia of Essential Oils*, years ago, where she showed that a number of brands labelled oregano oil were fraudulent. Those derived from *Thymus captitus* or Spanish thyme, including so-called Moroccan oregano oil, are unfit for human consumption.

One issue, here, is that fraudulent oregano oils are excessively high in thymol. In some cases, as demonstrated by gas chromatography these thymol levels can be as high as 30%, which is dangerous. This is a consequence of the direct toxicity of thymol to the heart and liver. Regarding the latter, in one case a product labeled "Oregano Oil" made by a major manufacturer caused a women to develop liver failure, manifested by jaundice and elevated liver enzymes, which is direct evidence of thymol toxicity.

Even when a reasonably natural oregano oil source is used, for instance, in imitation supplements, usually, the dose is too low. Such rather weak dosage supplements are not effective or only marginally so for the types of conditions mentioned in this book.

In the oregano oil 'industry' there is now much corruption. Do not be bamboozled and fooled by those who claim exceedingly high carvacrol levels. Those levels are never found in nature and surely never in amounts sufficient to put a product on the market. The maximum marketable level of carvacrol in a wild-source, all-natural oregano oil supplement is 84%, though, admittedly, there is a limited amount of such oil. Any claim higher than this percentage, such as 86% or greater, is likely a cheap imitation. This can be proven by careful analysis of wild extract through gas chromatography. Oregano oil containing carvacrol levels of 88% or higher is entirely corrupt, as such levels are an aberration not found in nature. Put simply, claims of carvacrol levels of 90% to 95% are proof of adulteration.

What about organic claims?

While an organic claim on oregano oil is generally positive it is not the most important issue. "Organic" may actually imply farm raised. This is less than ideal. Wild oregano never grows on farms, let alone soil. Instead, it grows in the mountains on rock or rock-infested soil, although it prefers rocks over dirt. The plant actually thrives on crumbled calcareous rock, a remnant of ancient sea beds. It is possible to even find oil of oregano labeled wild, also organic, when it isn't actually wild growing. Instead, it is wild-origin seeds or seed derivatives, which are through much manipulation merely grown on soil. In one case this author was contacted by one such grower, which claimed to manipulate the seeds in greenhouses in order to produce "high carvacrol cultivars." This was for the decided purpose of putting an altered, high- carvacrol 'standardized' oregano oil on the market. This explains the anomalies, like the imitation 88%-plus high carvacrol oregano oil that is on the market. Incredibly, this is purchased and then bottled, sold as "natural" or "wild, Mediterranean." Yet, it is neither natural nor wild in the least. Didn't anyone check the source to see if it is truly derived from wild-growing plants? Is no one paying attention to quality? Numerous companies do this, that is source, generically, while doing nothing to assure the source. They are not wild in the least and are, instead, fully farm-raised, even cloned. This is why a number of brands labeled Mediterranean, wild, or even organic are impotent compared to the truly wild, high-mountain variety. Thus, they are not tested and are not by any means safe for daily consumption.

Chapter Two

Chemistry of Wild Oregano

Wild oregano is a unique plant with potent phytochemistry virtually unmatched by any other. This makes it nature's most utilitarian and versatile plant medicine known. The aromatic complex itself has a wide range of phytochemicals. The distilled oil has its own panorama of active ingredients, and there are still yet other such active compounds in the hydrosol, known as the "juice." The fact that they contain different compounds explains the value of using them together.

Regarding oil of oregano this is produced by steam distillation. What results is a rather acrid, hot-tasting oil with an exceedingly pungent smell. At this point it is a crude distillate. This is the type ideal for human consumption. This is stated, since there are other types of 'oregano oils' on the market, which are not truly crude and unprocessed. These are the various refined and ultra-refined versions, which are commonly sold as actual wild or even organic oregano oil. Refined oils are also commonly available as aromatherapy grades as well as industrial and perfume grades. None of these are fit for human consumption.

Only the truly whole food, unprocessed oregano oil is optimal for consumption, particularly for daily or weekly intake. This type is never refined. It contains the whole complex of substances extracted in the basic, minimalized distillation process.

The difference is easy to confirm. This is through gas chromatography, which demonstrates a predictable profile: that of wild nature. In this profile, for instance, the one analyzed from a key, Mediterranean wild oregano oil, there are some 30 to 33 active ingredients. Through this, there is a synergy of ingredients, as found in nature. Adulterated or processed oregano oils, in contrast, are easy to identify. Upon being subjected to the same analysis they show an unexpected, if not bizarre, profile: as low as only four active ingredients, which means they are aberrations of nature. No doubt, this is a sign of corruption. The natural synergy in the oil is fully lost. In an independent analysis of some 30 oil of oregano 'brands' the number of active ingredients ranged from six to 33. Truly natural brands were in the range of 23 to 33 active components. Artificial or imitation ones ranged from 10 and lower.

What is the profile, then, of a truly whole food oil of wild oregano? The main density is in the form of a simple phenolic compound known as carvacrol. In a truly natural oregano oil, the levels of this powerful phenol range from 55% to 85%, the latter, higher number being rarer. On average, high-grade food-like oil of oregano ranges from 62% to 78% carvacrol, which is a sufficient density of this molecule. It truly is rare in nature to procure oregano oil with measurements of 80% or greater.

Carvacrol is a potent antioxidant and antiseptic. Yet, it is most efficient in its therapeutic actions when in combination with other key oregano oil active ingredients. A category of such active substances is the terpenes, found in the oil in a relatively high density. It is these substances, which are among the most powerful anti-inflammatory, as well as anti- pain, compounds known. These chemical complexes are also highly anti-tumor, for instance, limonene, well researched as an anticancer agent. One of the other primary terpenes in oregano oil is beta caryophyllene. According to a number of investigations this compound is one of the rare substances in nature with regenerative powers, in particular, for brain and nerve cells. Beta caryophyllene is a key active ingredient of a number of spice oils and is also the most biologically active compound of agricultural cannabis extract.

Oregano oil also contains pinene, a compound known to fight pain, while also aiding in increasing bone density. In the original brand sample borneol was found, which, like pinene, causes bone densification. There is a significant amount of linalool in high-grade, whole food oregano oils, which is a potent anti-tumor agent. Camphene is found in modest amounts, it, too, being highly anti-tumor. As well, 1, 8 cineol is found, which fights pain and inflammation and again acts as an antitumor agent. There is thymol, though, ideally in a low percentage, which acts in synergy with carvacrol as an antiparasitic agent, germicide, and antioxidant. So, it becomes clear that the focus on carvacrol alone, the antiseptic and antioxidant component, is insufficient.

In contrast, corrupt types of oregano oil supplements, even many produced by reputable dietary supplement manufacturers, lack these key synergists. Consider the following analyzed sample, containing only nine active ingredients. Camphene, limonene, linalool, and 1, 8 cineol, found routinely in whole food, wild samples, were all lacking in this sample. Yet, carvacrol was found at a level, incredibly, of 94%. It is no minor issue that these naturally occurring synergists are missing. Thus, there is no way this is a natural, true oregano oil. Yet, it is on the market as such. The fact is there is no 94% carvacrol-containing oregano oil in nature.

It is also no minor issue that companies are putting on the market suspect types of oregano oil, including those spiked or adulterated with synthetic carvacrol. This is precisely what occurred when the oregano oil market previously collapsed. In the 1930s adulterants were put in oregano oil and other essential oils, including synthetic phenols. This led to a number of fatalities, curtailing all interest in natural, phenolic-rich antiseptics.

The warning, then, is hereby sounded. Yet, it can be even more corrupt than was previously mentioned. In this case there are only six identifiable active ingredients found in gas chromatography, making this completely aberrant. In the analysis there was only carvacrol, thymol, borneol, trans caryophyllene, oxide of caryophyllene, and linalool. Where are the other naturally occurring terpenes? While the carvacrol is 'within range,' the thymol is too high, in fact, dangerously so at 10%. There is no way that this oil sample is derived from a completely natural-source wild oregano.

In addition, in true wild oregano oil there are substances known as long chain alcohols. Unlike ethyl alcohol these are natural phytochemicals with medicinal powers, acting primarily as anticancer agents. The terpenes and long chain alcohols are readily destroyed through adulteration.

In the water phase essence there are, also, novel compounds. This is a consequence of the interaction of water with the condensed oregano oil. The oxygen compounds in

water bind to the hydrogen bonds in the oregano molecules, making novel, highly oxygenated compounds.

This is another reason it is crucial to use only the whole food, crude extracts. As they are minimally processed, these extracts are rich in naturally occurring, molecularly bound oxygen. Such oxygen vitalizes the tissues, aiding cell metabolism and regeneration. Among the most oxygenated compounds in wild oregano are the terpenes, routinely corrupted and lost in adulterated versions, where the number of naturally occurring terpenes is greatly reduced.

Buyer beware—do not purchase or use oregano oil supplements unless they are guaranteed wild-source and unaltered with the full profile of chemical compounds, as occurs in nature. In particular, do not use such oils on a daily basis. Even so, all oregano oils will offer some degree of germ-killing powers. Yet, if they simultaneously disrupt the function of the gut and liver, the trade-off is poor. This is why the edible, daily use type from exclusively wild sources is emphasized. The truly whole food, wild-source oregano oil from true wild oregano species is entirely safe, including for consumption on a daily basis. This is true even in high doses, if such dosing is indicated.

Genetic source

There is another key issue when selecting wild oregano oil, and this is the genetic source. The plant originated in the deep Mediterranean, where it has grown for countless millions of years on the mountain slopes and tops. Oregano from all other regions are artifacts. For instance, types of oregano plants which grow in the Balkans, in Spain, in the south of France, on the Himalayan slopes, and throughout

North Africa. Yet, none of these are the true, medicinal spice: the original genetic source. For both safety and efficacy always use only truly Mediterranean-source wild oregano. These are the species which grow along the Fertile Crescent region from the Sinai up and through Anatolia. It is precisely such types of wild oregano that have been used by humanity for countless generations without any untoward effects and, rather, with the utmost positive benefits, including the eradication of potentially deadly diseases.

False high carvacrol claims

The occurrence of exceptionally high carvacrol levels in nature is relatively rare. This is in respect to levels in wild plants. Carvacrol amounts can be manipulated, for instance, through selective cloning. This is surely not natural. Even so, such cloning is commonly done today. The purpose is to create high carvacrol-producing biotypes for making extracted oil. This is done to bamboozle the public, that is 'Ours is higher in carvacrol than the competing brand' and similar marketing hype.

There are a number of companies which are doing this, and which are strictly using farm-raised oregano as the source for the creation of the high carvacrol lines. In nature oregano never grows on farms. Rather, it thrives exclusively in the wild, growing on the rocky slopes of high mountains. For instance, one company with a significant Internet profile and various testimonials claims a minimum of 86% carvacrol. Knowing this is virtually impossible to find in the wild the Website was investigated. It turns out that this 'Greek oregano' touted as from the species O. heraculoticum is strictly farm-raised: at unnaturally low elevation. Such

oregano is vulnerable to attack by organisms, including mold. If it is grown in an entirely unnatural environment, and, thus, the profile is aberrant. Regardless, why purchase farm-raised oregano when the truly wild type, the one produced by the vast powers of nature, is available? In addition, unlike the truly wild varieties the oil derived from farm-raised oregano, whether high or low carvacrol, cannot be deemed safe for daily consumption.

Too, if a company was legitimate in the goal of actually producing high-quality natural medicines, why would any such an entity attempt to mimic a wild plant by merely growing it, agriculturally, creating an abnormal chemical profile? Once again, do not consume farm-raised oregano as a daily supplement or as the basis for the protocols in this book.

Other false carvacrol claims are made, as mentioned, through the addition of synthetic chemicals. Still others claim high levels, but upon gas chromatographic analysis these claims do not hold up. Of course, all such pseudo-high carvacrol supplements, particularly the farm-raised types, are cheaper than the true, wild-source oil where carvacrol exclusively is not emphasized. For quality oregano oil it's not the carvacrol levels alone that's the issue. It is the fact that the oregano oil must be derived exclusively from wild plants and that the genetic source must be original to those plants. Through this, there is absolute safety, even in high doses. Most importantly, such wild-source oregano oil is the most potent of all as a therapeutic intervention against degenerative disease.

Chapter Three

The Premier Antioxidant

Antioxidants are in the news, and people are focusing on them, legitimately so. Routinely, individuals are consuming antioxidant-rich fruit and vegetables, as well as various supplements, as a means of protection: as an essential tool for blocking the aging process and in the prevention of disease. Yet, the greatest, most potent antioxidant known is being virtually neglected. This is wild oregano and its extracts, which are far more powerful in their antioxidative capacities than any known fruit, mushroom, or vegetable and, in fact, more so than any other herbal medicine.

It was the USDA that confirmed this, finding that simple oregano spice was the most aggressive antioxidant of all commonly consumed foods. It was, they discovered, 42 times more potent at quenching potentially dangerous free radicals than apple skins. Regarding the oil, ORAC testing demonstrates that no common herb or food can compare. With an ORAC free radical quenching value of 3000, in comparison, blueberries are only 30, meaning that oregano oil is 100 times more potent. Even the plain spice is superior to most fruit, with an ORAC level four-fold greater than blueberries.

There are a number of novel substances within the oil that account for this immense antioxidant capacity. These substances include carvacrol and also caryophyllene. The highly aggressive molecule carvacrol vigorously traps free radicals of all types, including the exceedingly destructive hydroxyl radical. Beta caryophyllene, in particular, protects brain and nerve cells from oxidative damage, while also having the capacity to regenerate them once they are damaged and/or destroyed. As well, linalool and limonene, also found in wild oregano oil, are neuron regenerating agents.

This issue of the multiplicity of natural compounds in wild oregano cannot be stressed enough. This is because there are now on the market a number of false or imitation oregano oils, which are deficient: which fail to provide this rich diversity of compounds. It is these other diverse compounds besides carvacrol that largely account for its immense antioxidant capacities. In addition to the caryophyllenes consider the other terpenes which account for its free radical scavenging activity and antioxidant capacities. Among these are novel compounds such as camphene, hydrat, along with beta pinene, terpinen-4-ol, and alpha terpinene. Consider, too, the highly medicinal and fully edible citrus-like terpenes limonene and linalool. For optimal efficacy, ideally, all such terpenes or similar terpene-based molecules must be present in the whole, crude wild oregano complex.

There is yet another novel power of wild oregano oil. This relates to the key cellular antioxidant, glutathione. The intake of the oil greatly induces internal production of this antioxidant compound, both in the liver and the cells at-large.

In the liver there is a special type of this molecule, which is required for the survival of every cell in its tissues. Known as glutathione-S-transferase this molecule is the key one for assisting the liver in the detoxification of potentially poisonous compounds. In fact, all cleansing and detoxification in the tissues is dependent upon it. This is why oregano oil is such a potent antidote for chemical poisoning, including intoxication by herbicides, pesticides, petrochemicals, mycotoxins, heavy metals, and venom. Wild oregano oil has, thus, several mechanisms of action against poisoning. It directly neutralizes poisonous chemicals, oxidizing them, while also bolstering the internal detoxification pathways. Simultaneously, it blocks the typical oxidative damage that occurs from exposure to such chemicals. No other substance can compare to its diverse powers in the protection of the body from toxins. This demonstrates that for any detoxification plan wild oregano is essential therapy. Both the steam distilled oil and the supercritical extract are potent glutathione inducing agents.

This induction of glutathione is a novel property of this oil. The importance of this cannot be understated. Glutathione is found in all cells of the body and in dense amounts within vulnerable, organs, like the liver, kidneys, spleen, prostate, and endocrine glands. Through the intake of a truly food-grade, highly metabolically active, edible oil of oregano, essentially, all such organs are protected from degeneration. The fact is glutathione is the front-line defense within the cells from metabolic oxidative damage, the type of toxicity that leads to degenerative disease.

It is more than merely this. According to Indian investigators all the body's antioxidative enzymes are enhanced by oregano oil therapy. In this study it was determined that in mice exposed to a potent hydrocarbon carcinogen, dimethylhydrazine, a compound, essentially, similar to airline fuel there was a decline in the key protective enzymes: superoxide dismutase, catalase, glutathione peroxidase, and glutathione-S-transferase. This decline was fully reversed through oregano supplementation. The positive benefits were of such a degree that the researchers suggested the herb is preventive against colon cancer. One of the main reasons for this action is not merely carvacrol but also the various actions of the whole food terpenes, including caryophyllene.

Even on the skin wild oregano oil is protective, once again, because of a dual mechanism of direct antioxidative actions, along with that crucial indirect element, the induction of glutathione. This is why oil of wild oregano is unmatched as a full body antioxidant for protecting the tissue against the ravages of degenerative diseases.

A number of other spice oils and spice-like complexes offer these powers. Spices and their oils capable of inducing the production of glutathione include *Rhus coriaria*, cumin, fennel, bay leaf, rosemary, turmeric, and sage. For optimal health all such spices and/or their extracts should be routinely included in the diet.

Regarding wild oregano there is significant data supporting its antioxidant powers. Bendini and his group publishing in the *Italian Journal of Food Science* determined that a leaf extract in alcohol was a potent inhibitor of lipid oxidation, the type that occurs within human cell walls. It is a compelling finding, because it implies that the spice blocks cellular decay and degeneration. This was confirmed by Turkish investigators, who found, definitively, that oil of oregano prevents oxidation of lipid components when added to meat and other foods in rather small amounts. It simply halted any oxidation that would be expected to occur in

polyunsaturated fats. The greatest effect at preservation occurred when animals were fed the essential oil in the daily diet, once again demonstrating the powers of this spice oil complex for daily use.

In fact, the edible type is so versatile that it must be regarded as the most crucial natural medicine known for the protection of all organ systems, including highly vulnerable ones, like the liver and kidneys. This brings up the issue of toxicity concerns. There are those who claim that oregano oil cannot be taken regularly, because of the possibility of liver or kidney toxicity. While this may be true of imitation brands, the so-called cheap or inferior adulterations, it is certainly not the case with the wild, food-based oil. In fact, it is the opposite effect, which is that it is therapeutic for disorders of these two delicate excretory organs. This is because of its regenerative powers and its capacity to induce glutathione synthesis, which is needed for tissue repair after trauma or toxicity. In other words, if a person suffered a sudden assault to the liver and/or kidneys edible, daily use oregano oil would be an ideal treatment, specifically the highly regarded, original brand that is commonly consumed by people in the know.

Consider the findings of Turkish investigators publishing in *Phytomedicine*. The researchers did the untenable, which was to cut out a portion of the livers of test rats, a great stress upon their systems, and then challenge these livers with carvacrol (extracted from oregano oil). Was there any toxicity? In fact, it was the opposite. Impressively, the carvacrol "increased the liver regeneration rate." Still other investigators have found that in test animals when artificial ischemia was produced, leading to oxidative damage, carvacrol was hepatoprotective. Baser of Andalou

University has deemed oregano oil to be a significant "antihepatotoxic" agent, meaning, in fact, it should be given in the event of liver intoxication. Therefore, those who claim that true oregano oil is poisonous or that, somehow, it can cause liver damage are erroneous.

Once again, merely because of a lack of knowledge plus fear, people are neglecting the most potent, versatile antioxidant known. Through ignorance, individuals have spread the misinformation that wild oregano is unsafe for regular or long-term use. This is patently false. It is the opposite, which is that it is harmful to the body *not* to use it as a result of the ravages of aging: free radical formation, cellular degeneration, oxidative damage, infectious assault, viral invasion, and far more. This has been demonstrated in a number of scientific studies. It has also been shown that wild oregano, including the extracted oil, is just as safe as other common food-like antioxidants such as vitamin E and vitamin C. In fact, in one study done on chicken thigh meat it was found that wild oregano enhances naturally occurring antioxidants. It is known that thigh meat is the most susceptible part of the chicken flesh to oxidation, even though it has a dense amount of alpha tocopherol. Curiously, during freezing the levels of this vitamin in chicken meat declines over time. Supplementation with oregano oil increased the retention of vitamin E in the meat significantly, which means it prevented it from degrading.

Yet, in this research something incredible was found. It was determined that oil of oregano had a "much higher level of total antioxidant activity at some 2.5 million antioxidant equivalents compared to vitamin E at about 39,000. In other research it was found that, largely because of this exceedingly potent antioxidant potential, oil of oregano proved to be an

anti-inflammatory agent, even curbing inflammation in the gut linings of test animals, in this case, swine. Here, it curtailed the toxicity of oxygen radicals, which develop in animal intestines as a result of pathogen overload.

In consequence an interesting comment was made. In contrast to drugs the oregano oil is not only safe and non- toxic to animal cell linings but it also fails to "leave residues in the environment." Plus, unlike drugs, it is synergistic with the naturally occurring antioxidants, like vitamins C, A, and E. This synergy occurs both in food and in living animal tissue. After all, it's a food. What harm could there be in daily, routine consumption or for that matter via the consumption of large quantities: as long as it is the edible, daily use type?

It is all because wild oregano extracts represent a rare biological chemistry. This is the capacity to both destroy noxious germs, while also halting the standard consequence of combating infection: free radical generation. This double mechanism makes, for instance, wild oregano oil unique, far more so than antibiotics or any other pharmaceutically- based germ killers. As well, while it is purging germs and quenching free radicals it is simultaneously halting inflammation. This is a triplicate mechanism. No pharmaceutical drug, in fact, legions of them can achieve this.

Pain relief

There is yet another little-known property of wild oregano oil, in fact, all types of oregano supplements. This is the capacity to ease and relieve pain. There are a number of mechanisms which account for this power. Carvacrol itself has significant analgesic properties. In one animal study conducted by Turkish investigators carvacrol-rich wild oregano oil was found to modulate pain to such a degree that it was equally effective compared to non-steroidal anti-inflammatory agents and some one-third as potent as morphine. Additionally, the terpenes in wild oregano offer significant pain-relieving properties, for instance, beta caryophyllene and trans caryophyllene, which are dietary cannabinoids. These terpenes help modulate nerve chemistry, easing the sensations of pain while also helping to curb inflammation. Such pain-killing properties are demonstrated through both topical and internal use. The fact is the pain-easing properties are so significant that it can be regarded as the most dependable topical balm known.

There is yet another capacity of this spice complex for combating pain, including the deep-seated type, like bone pain. This is in relation to the powers of wild oregano active ingredients relative to the bones. The spice complex contains compounds which directly affect the bone matrix, curbing inflammation and, therefore, pain. These compounds, the phenolic substances, such as carvacrol, and also the terpenes, such as the caryophyllenes and pinenes, exert significant capacities for building the health of the bones. In fact, wild oregano in all its forms, the whole, crude herb, the oil, and the aromatic essence, have direct, potent actions on bone tissue. This is to such a degree that they are dependable complexes for significantly increasing bone density. This is demonstrated by the work of Muhlbauer, who showed that certain spices dramatically increase bone remodeling, that is they reverse losses in this tissue, while increasing the laying down of new bone. It is only the spices and similar phytochemical complexes that can achieve this. By doing so pain throughout the body is greatly diminished, as is the vulnerability to skeletal injury and fractures. Only oregano complexes rich in the various terpenes, including beta caryophyllene, offer such significant powers.

Chapter Four

The Why Behind Wild Oregano Oil

Truly wild oregano oil is an extremely valuable natural medicine. It can save humankind from the ravages of countless diseases, including a number of potentially fatal ones, like autoimmune disorders, heart disease, blood poisoning, gangrene, and diabetes as well as, to a degree, cancer. What could be more profound and truly invaluable than this?

It is also the most crucial preventive for a variety of infectious diseases, including the killer drug-resistant types. Too, it is a categorical cure for the common cold and also the flu. Additionally, it is a powerhouse against pneumonia and all other serious lung infections. Make no mistake nothing, whether natural or synthetic, can surpass its beneficial actions for needy, vulnerable humankind.

Thus, much credit must be given to those responsible for this, who bravely originated the wild oregano oil movement against all odds.

The responsible parties have brought forth to humankind a novel type of therapy that was never before realized or utilized. People who have merely copied the trend are not the innovators. For instance, no one knew that wild oregano oil fully obliterates the cold and flu viruses, that is until these findings were published in the aforementioned book. As well, there was no knowledge of its immense value in bronchitis, which it obliterates, a condition deemed by medicine as incurable. Regarding sinus conditions no one knew that it fully eradicates these, taken internally and also applied into the nostrils and sinus cavities. Yet another innovation in this regard was the creation of a sinus spray with wild oils of oregano, bay leaf, and sage, a major advancement, effective to the extreme. As well, no company or entity prior had done any significant research on wild oregano's potent antiviral properties, for instance, versus the cold and flu viruses. The research in question, published in *Antiviral Research*, proves that wild oregano oil, particularly the super-strength form and also as a component of the multiple spice oil complex with oil of wild sage plus cumin and cinnamon oils, decimates cold and flu viruses. This oil complex was so potent that even its mere presence in cell culture preventing any regrowth of the viruses.

So, credit must be given where it is due: to those who bravely brought this forward. This is a positive element, since it aids in the selection of a top-quality supplement rather than those imitation brands, never based on scientific investigation.

Wild oregano oil has reached the federal level. The FDA has shown an interest in wild oregano oil. This was through a series of studies it funded at the University of Tennessee- Knoxville. Lead research, F. Ann Draughn, had this to say about the FDA initiative, which involved some $450,000 of US taxpayer monies. It was the fact that the FDA and her team would seek to prove the untenable: that the intake of oregano oil or, for that matter, any spice for purposes of health advancement "was a useless endeavor." She would prove it, she said, through the study. Instead, incredibly, the opposite occurred.

In a personal interview the investigator said that she and her team 'tried everything' to prove, in particular, oregano oil was a fraud, especially in regard to its germ- killing properties. She sent the oil into the lab, testing it against various pathogens. It categorically obliterated them. Frustrated and finding this unbelievable, she did it again, with the same result. At that time, she reported, she had excoriated her lab tech, saying she had contaminated the test with, perhaps, chlorinated water, which the tech vehemently denied. The third time was, as it is said, "a charm," as it is said, since, once again, the oil wiped out the germs. The study was ultimately published in the *Journal of Food Science*, where, the investigators concluded, oregano oil is so effective it should be turned into a drug. Clearly, then, it was determined that all previous claims regarding oregano oils powers were hardly baseless and, rather, were highly substantial.

Mediterranean sourced oregano oil is the subject of carefully controlled scientific studies in peer- review journals. This original type is also the only one produced through a rigid quality control system, operated and coordinated to the fullest degree, from the handpicking of the wild spice to its careful, minimalist extraction through steam distillation and then, ultimately, its blending and bottling in the correct formulation in the United States. In this regard, once again, it has done the research, performing its landmark scientific study at Georgetown University, one that has brought forth medical proof of not only wild oregano oil's immense therapeutic powers but also its high degree of safety. Through such efforts formulations have been created which are optimal for human and animal use. Even so, this is not an endorsement of any brand for the treatment of medical diseases. Rather, it is merely factual information for the benefit of the reader to in order to make sound purchasing decisions for procuring the highest quality supplements possible.

The Georgetown University study, published in *Molecular and Cellar Biochemistry,* demonstrated a number of findings, including:

- the fact that essential oil of oregano in a neat or undiluted form is not fit for human consumption and, particularly, animal consumption internally

- that the edible, daily use form as an extra virgin olive oil emulsion is fit for human and animal intake and in an animal model saved the lives of test mice from candida yeast infection equally to potent drugs

- that the edible, daily use type of wild oregano oil demonstrated no toxicity to test animals, even upon the intake of significant doses and that, rather, its intake proved lifesaving

- that synthetic forms of oregano oil, notably those tainted with chemically produced carvacrol, while effective as germicides, do have a degree of toxicity

The study was conducted to determine if wild oregano oil would clear pathogenic yeasts from the test animal tissues as well as common drugs; the oil did so efficiently, which astonished the medically oriented investigators. This led to a flurry of research by other investigators, which fully confirmed the findings.

In the USA-based research described here, it should be noted, the whole food, wild oregano complex was the only type used. Curiously, it has resulted in aggressive research in animal husbandry, leading to the application of oregano oil as an alternative to antibiotics. Today, because of these original research efforts, such as the Georgetown findings and that published in *Antiviral Research*, major meat producers, such as Purdue Chicken, now use in feeding lines oregano oil instead of potentially dangerous drugs.

The Georgetown research is highly significant in its implications for humans. Here, the value of oregano oil for combating candida-induced conditions was elucidated. Such candida-based syndromes include immune deficiency disorders, endometriosis, infertility, vaginitis, yeast syndrome, PMS, chronic fatigue syndrome, fibromyalgia, Crohn's disease, and irritable bowel syndrome. The fact is the revelation led to a virtual research movement on spice oil-based candida treatments, with investigators, globally, confirming the findings.

Yeast is a major cause of human ailments and is a particularly devastating factor in female disorders. It can categorically cause infertility as well as bizarre, difficult to diagnose syndromes such as interstitial cystitis and lupus. It can also cause infertility in men as well as prostate disorders. Wild oregano oil can be relied upon by all who suffer these syndromes with major benefits largely because it purges the primary cause, which is fungal infestation. As well, company-sponsored research proves it effective against a number of pathogenic bacteria, including staph and tuberculosis species.

It must be reiterated. Wild oregano oil is also an efficient antiviral agent. This is crucial, since there is no drug known which has such powers. It was Siddiqui and his group publishing in *Medical Science Research* who demonstrated the mechanism. When the oil interacted with the viral coating, a most compelling finding was made under electron microscopy. Incredibly, it disintegrated this coating, killing the viruses. As mentioned previously this was confirmed by the work of Ijaz, Ingram, and co-workers, where oregano oil killed 99.7% or greater of cold and flu viruses in cell culture, once again through dissolving the viral membrane. No drug known has this capacity even to the most minute degree. This is a life-saving revelation, as there is no pharmaceutical agent capable of such a broad-spectrum action against viral pathogens.

There is another great 'why' for this spice complex. Wild oregano, including its extracted oil and the aromatic hydrosol, is a food. This makes it the most novel natural medicine conceivable, particularly in respect to its medicinal properties. It is a most incredible feat, one that could only be a consequence of the Divine hand. After all, it's a food-based germ killer and immune potentiator. Yet, it is also an edible anti-inflammatory agent, anti-pain complex, antitussive or anti-cough agent, antihistamine, and antioxidant. Because it is a food it is a most invaluable natural medicine for human use known. Moreover, it is the most potent natural remedy available for combating the ravages of degenerative disease. Even in incredibly large doses there is no toxicity. Yet, this is true only of the 100% whole food, Mediterranean-source wild oregano. Cheaper imitations cannot be taken with such impunity.

As the true wild oregano oil is so safe and versatile it is, thus, the ideal natural medicine for stubborn conditions, where large dosing is necessary. With these resistant conditions, like toenail fungus, Lyme disease, autoimmune disorders, chronic fatigue syndrome, and chronic viral syndromes, few other therapies are available. For the sake of human health nothing could be more superior to this.

There is another issue, which is sustainability and environmentalism. Oregano and its extracts are biodegradable. Thus, unlike drugs, they leave no negative environmental impact upon the earth. Consider, in contrast, antibiotics, which cause vast pollution of the environment as well as, upon ingestion, much drug toxicity. The pollution is so extreme that, typically, residues of pharmaceutical drugs are found in city drinking water and even in well water.

A number of antibiotics may even cause permanent liver and kidney damage, for instance, erythromycin and aminoglycosides. There is also the issue of the induction of potentially fatal drug-resistant germs, which is the greatest debacle of all. This is no minor issue, as in the United States alone these drug-induced infections are responsible for tens of millions of illnesses yearly. Horrifically, in the USA alone deaths from the overuse of antibiotics, both from direct toxicity and, in particular, induction of drug resistant pathogens, may amount to as high as 300,000 per year.

In animals overuse of antibiotics causes great disturbances in their health and also serious diseases, while also leading to toxicity in those who eat the corrupted tissue. None of this occurs with wild oregano therapy. In fact, when fed to farm animals, it is the opposite, because it makes their tissues healthier. Additionally, pets, are highly vulnerable to a variety of conditions which oregano therapy can both treat and prevent.

In contrast to single drugs wild oregano oil is a complex of active ingredients, in some cases up to 33 different synergistic components. Higher carvacrol types of wild oregano oil may contain as many as 22 active components. The synergy of all these active elements is what makes wild oregano oil unique compared to drugs, including antibiotics. Because of the multiplicity of elements microbial resistance is virtually unknown. Moreover, the mechanism of action prevents this. For instance, carvacrol, the primary active ingredient, has a mechanism of action which the germs cannot resist. It destroys their cell coating, in the case of viruses, for instance, disintegrating it. With bacteria, the cell walls are, essentially, melted.

High carvacrol can be of value. Yet, there is a degree of caution here. A number of unscrupulous purveyors have put on the market oregano oil with synthetic carvacrol or that derived from cloned, farmed raised types with artificially high levels of this crucial component. This is particularly true of all companies which claim carvacrol levels above 88%. There is no such wild oregano oil with these levels in nature.

Now, there is available an ultra-carvacrol-rich oil of wild oregano that is 100% wild and which contains the highest naturally occurring density of this substance possible. This ultra-rich formula is highly potent and may be relied upon for tough, stubborn conditions. A powerful antiseptic it is also an invaluable complex for combating pain and inflammation syndromes, as carvacrol is one of the most vigorous anti-pain substances known. This ultra-rich formula has an exceptionally robust taste and aroma and is itself highly pleasing to the senses, that is the senses involved in aiding relaxation and combating stress. Yet, what could be more relaxing that to be free of all pain and agony? Ultra carvacrol-rich oregano oil, in this case 84% or higher, is also highly exceptionally effective against skin diseases. This includes extreme power against warts, skin boils, tags, age spots, moles, and even skin cancer.

For a vast number of reasons wild oregano is the essential choice for all humanity. It is in a category all its own. By no means does any other substance have such a broad-spectrum of applications. Let anyone name it. What other therapeutic substance can be relied upon for countless dozens of uses? What else can be used successfully and routinely for virtually all major health conditions? So, let us review the 101 uses and much more, organized into various categories.

Chapter Five

Respiratory System

Regarding the respiratory system wild oregano and its extracts are the premier of all natural medicines. Virtually every respiratory ailment known will succumb to therapeutic intervention through the intake of high-quality wild oregano oil as well as the aromatic water-phase essence. The conditions covered in this section alone reveal the incredibly immense value of wild oregano oil for human health. No wonder it is the only plant medicine described in biblical lore as a 'purging herb,' that is, essentially, a cure- all. In antiquity to purge most likely meant to 'clean' the body not of mere toxins but, rather, of dangerous pathogens. In that era this is what was most deadly to the people. The scriptural statement is correct, God be praised, because this is precisely what wild oregano achieves.

Even so, by no means can the numerous imitation brands be recommended for use in the conditions mentioned, here, or for the scope of intake recommended. In this regard in some cases relatively large doses are recommended. Only the truly wild, Mediterranean-source oregano oil derived from the edible spice can be given in such doses. It is tested and known to be safe for this degree of internal consumption. In this regard beware of imitations, especially those made from farm-raised, genetically altered/cloned, and/or GMO-tainted oregano. For instance, one popular brand is infested with GM soy lecithin. Such lecithin is poisonous, accounting for gastrointestinal toxicity reported by users.

Truly wild, Mediterranean-source oil of oregano is highly effective against all respiratory disorders as well as allergic reactions. It is also a potent therapy for lung toxicity as occurs from chemical exposure. Even asbestosis responds to its therapeutic powers. In many cases it is so effective than no other medicine is needed. The following are the various respiratory, allergic, and sinus conditions which are known to respond positively to wild oregano oil therapy:

Colds/flu

It was primarily oil of wild oregano, as well as the juice/essence, which revolutionized modern treatment for colds and flu. In particular, through the ingestion of the daily use oregano oil people with these conditions responded dramatically. The crude herbal complex with *Rhus coriaria* also proved effective, particularly in children. In many cases the oil alone simply shut down the cold/flu reaction, halting all symptoms in a few hours or less or at least cutting the duration of symptoms by 50%. Moreover, with daily or routine use of the oil, essence, and/or whole food complex there was another medical breakthrough. Colds and flu were prevented from occurring, something that no other therapeutic agents had ever been able to achieve. For human beings this leads to a

great reduction in the disease burden, a most impressive and positive achievement. The consequence is a greater degree of productivity:

for society at-large. Those responsible should be given a reward for this achievement.

Even so, common medical therapies for colds and flu cannot compare. Consider the flu vaccine. This involves the injection of live flu viruses into the body, which itself can result in much disease. How can this compare to actually killing viruses, thus safely eliminating the symptoms?

Treatment protocol

Take the oil of wild oregano, ideally as drops under the tongue, five or more drops multiple times daily, in fact, as often as is necessary to eliminate the symptoms. As well, rub the oil on the bottoms of the feet and also about the upper chest, with major emphasis on the areas of lymphatic drainage about the clavicles. Also, rub the oil up and down the spine, as noxious viruses may readily hide within the spinal fluids.

Take the whole food, crude herb complex with *Rhus coriaria,* two capsules several times daily, whole food vitamin C complex with the combination of wild camu camu and acerola and the juice or essence of wild oregano, a tablespoon multiple times daily.

Bronchitis

While it is little realized bronchitis is caused not by bacteria or viruses but, rather, fungi. The fungi infect the bronchial tubes, causing inflammation and irritation. The organisms involved are the typical ones found in the air and surfaces: black mold, greenish mold, and brown rust mold. Oil of wild oregano is so potent for this condition that no other herbal medicine is required. It obliterates the actively growing molds, also destroying any embedded spores. Its powers are facilitated by the simultaneous intake of the juice of wild oregano. As well, in some cases the condition is aggravated by food intolerance such as allergic reactivity to wheat, rye, dairy products, refined sugar, aspartame, corn products, among other foods/substances.

Treatment protocol

Take the oil of wild oregano daily, ideally as drops under the tongue, five to ten drops under the tongue multiple times daily until the condition is reversed.

Optional

Take the juice or essence of wild oregano, one or more tablespoon twice daily, along with whole food vitamin A complex from wild sockeye salmon oil, three capsules twice daily.

Sinusitis

With this condition the perpetrating factor is almost always fungi, notably molds. The molds infect the deep recesses of the sinus cavities, leading to much inflammation, swelling, and pain. In medicine the wrong approach is taken, which is antibiotics and surgery. This serves no good purpose and, in fact, drives the infection deeper into the tissues. It is through the original whole food, daily use wild oregano oil that the true cause of sinusitis was proven, as the intake of this oil obliterates this condition. That is because now it is known that rather than bacteria it is mold which causes this condition. This led to significant research, including a prominent Mayo Clinic study where it was found that in 95% of all patients suffering from chronic sinus conditions there is mold infestation within the sinus cavities. In some cases, up to eight different molds were found to infect simultaneously in the test subjects' nasal and sinus cavities.

Treatment protocol

Take the oil of wild oregano, ideally as drops under the tongue, five or more drops three times daily. As well, apply a small amount of the oil on a Q-Tip and place up the medial aspect of the nose along the nasal septum, avoiding the sensitive outer nasal membrane.

Optional (but highly recommended)

Nasal spray consisting of a sea salt/saline base with oils of wild oregano, sage, and bay leaf, along with the whole food, wild cod or sockeye salmon oil as a source of vitamin A, two or more capsules twice daily.

Pneumonia

Regardless of the cause, that is bacteria, viruses, or fungi, pneumonia is curable with wild oregano oil therapy. Prior to this revelation there was no dependable natural remedy available that would reverse this disease. This is particularly crucial, since in many cases orthodox medical therapy, such as antibiotics, fails to resolve it. In hospitalized patients' pneumonia is a major debacle, acting as a primary cause of death. This could be routinely prevented through the aggressive intake of the oil, along with the aromatic essence.

Treatment protocol

Take the oil of wild oregano daily, five to ten drops multiple times daily, as often as necessary to reverse the syndrome. For severe cough or in tough cases also consume the juice of wild oregano, two tablespoons twice daily.

Optional

Take the whole food vitamin C complex, two capsules twice daily.

Sore throat/tonsillitis

Usually caused by bacteria sore throat and/or tonsillitis can also be caused by viruses and fungi, including black mold. As well, toxic reactions to allergens can lead to both these conditions. Sudden onset sore throat with swollen glands is usually viral or bacterial in origin. In all cases oil of wild oregano, taken sublingually or in juice/water, quickly obliterates the pathogens, eliminating all symptoms.

Treatment protocol

Take the oil of wild oregano daily, five or more drops multiple times per day. Hold the dose under the tongue as long as possible. Also, allow it to coat the back of the throat. Use also a wild oregano-based spray, misting it into the back of the throat as often as needed.

Mastoiditis

In this condition the mastoid process of the ear area becomes infected, usually by bacteria but also in some cases by fungi and yeasts. Mastoiditis is often associated with ear infections and earaches.

Treatment protocol

Take the oil of wild oregano daily, five or more drops multiple times per day. Also apply the oil to the mastoid process, that is the boney prominence just below the ear lobe, as often as possible. Do this repeatedly until the condition is resolved.

Earache

For this condition there is nothing superior to this therapy. Earaches are often caused by toxic reactions to foods and beverages, while few people realize it. As well, mold toxicity is a perpetrator, as is infestation by candida. Moreover, antibiotic therapy, which perpetrates yeast infection, is a major cause of earaches. As well, the oil is the optimal treatment for irritation in the ear canal such as pressure or itchy ears. Here, it can be taken as drops under the tongue or applied just in the outer aspect of the ear canal.

Treatment protocol

Take the oil of wild oregano daily, ideally as drops under the tongue, a few drops three times daily. Also, rub the oil all about the outer ear, behind the ear, and on the tragus or soft, hanging tissue. A drop or two can be put on a Q-Tip and held against the outer section of the ear canal. The sinus-oregano & bay leaf oil-based spray can also be used as ear drops.

Hay fever and allergic rhinitis

These are among the easiest conditions to reverse. All that is necessary is the intake of wild oregano, ideally both as the oil and the whole food crushed herb with *Rhus coriaria*. These conditions are related, certainly, in part to allergy, but they are also caused by mold reactions and in the case of allergic rhinitis, mold infection. Oil of oregano and the food- based crushed herbal capsules are not only antifungal but are also powerful antihistamines. Buffered whole food vitamin C free of all GMOs is also a potent antihistamine effective against these conditions.

Treatment protocol

Take the oil of wild oregano, ideally as drops under the tongue, five or more drops twice daily. Also, consume the highly antihistaminic whole food vitamin C complex with the combination of wild camu camu, acerola, and rose hips, one or more capsules twice daily. Strictly avoid the consumption of GMO-tainted synthetic vitamin C, labeled as ascorbic acid on most supplements.

Snotty nose (in children)

Children should never suffer from this condition. A snotty- nosed child is one who suffers a derangement of the immune system as well as allergic intolerance. This is a sign of compromised immunity in children as well as nutritional deficiency. One major dilemma is vaccine intoxication, which fully destabilizes the immune system, leading to bronchial, nasal, and congestion disorders.

Treatment protocol

Take the oil of wild oregano daily, ideally as drops under the tongue, two or more drops twice daily. Also, rub the oil on the bottom of the child's feet and also up and down the shins and up and down the spine.

Optional

Consume whole food, all-natural wild vitamin C powder consisting of wild camu camu, acerola, and rose hips, half tsp. daily.

Chronic or irritating cough

In all cases of chronic cough wild oil of oregano is the preferred natural medicine. No cough can resist its powers. It is the most potent antitussive agent known. It is also a mucolytic agent, meaning it splits up and dissolves

excessive mucous deposits. Additionally, the juice of wild oregano is highly effective versus cough and is an essential part of this therapy.

Treatment protocol

Take the oil of wild oregano, ideally as drops under the tongue, three to five drops as often as necessary. Also, rub the oil on the bottoms of the feet and up and down the shins. As well, consume the juice of wild oregano, a tablespoon or two daily.

Optional

Whole food, all-natural wild-source vitamin C powder made with wild camu camu and acerola, half tsp. daily, along with whole food, wild cod or sockeye salmon oil as a source of naturally occurring vitamins A and D, two or more capsules twice daily.

Tuberculosis and cystic fibrosis

These are placed together, since they are regarded as incurable respiratory diseases, although in both there is often extension to other organs, notably the skin and digestive tract. There is an international resurgence of this disease with most cases remaining indolent and undiagnosed. Signs of undiagnosed TB include weight loss, chronic cough, fatigue, loss of appetite, night sweats, foamy or blood-streaked mucous when coughing, rising body temperature in the afternoon up until about 10:00 p.m., and, occasionally, bizarre skin lesions.

Treatment protocol

Take the super-strength oil of wild oregano daily, ideally as drops under the tongue, 10 or more drops three times daily. In extreme cases take 20 or more drops four or more times daily until the condition is stabilized and resolved, dropping the dose thereafter to 10 to 20 drops twice daily.

Optional

The oil works best if combined with juice of oregano, an ounce twice daily, and the multiple spice oil-based capsules, three capsules three times daily, along with a whole food, non-synthetic vitamin pack, at least one packet daily as well as whole food, natural source vitamin C (not ascorbic acid), two capsules twice daily.

Asbestosis

In this condition asbestos fibers accumulate in the lower poles of the lungs, causing great irritation and inflammation. This ultimately leads to chronic lung disease and, eventually, lung cancer, largely in the form of mesothelioma. The condition is reversible, since wild oregano oil dissolves the fibers, eliminating the source of the inflammation and causing a remission in the cancer.

Treatment protocol

Take the oil of wild oregano, ideally in the super-strength form, 20 drops three or more times daily. Also, consume the juice or essence of wild oregano, one ounce twice daily. Note: in some cases, the results are so dramatic that residues of the asbestos matter are coughed-up.

Nasal polyps

Nasal polyps are related to irritation of the nasal membranes, usually as a result of mold infestation. They are also caused by vitamin A deficiency as well as a deficit of vitamin C. To reverse this condition, it is essential to reduce the inflammation within the nasal cavity, while also correcting the nutritional deficiencies. The inflammation is most readily resolved through a combination of topical and internal use of oil of wild oregano.

Treatment protocol

Take the oil of wild oregano daily, ideally as drops under the tongue, five to ten drops twice daily. Also use the sinus-oregano spray, squirting large amounts into both nostrils twice daily. As well, the oil can be applied to a Q-Tip and slid up the nostrils along the medial aspect of the nose, along the septum, avoiding the more sensitive outer nasal membrane, to attempt to shrink the polyps.

Optional

Consume fatty wild cod or sockeye salmon oil as source of truly whole food vitamin A, three or more capsules twice daily or two teaspoons daily.

Pleurisy and/or collapsed lung

The main perpetrator of pleurisy and/or collapsed lung is tuberculosis. Another factor is black mold infection. In this condition there is infection of the pleural cavity, which makes it difficult or painful to take a deep breath. The condition may also be related to a deficiency of the lung- supporting nutrient, vitamin A.

Treatment protocol

Take the oil of wild oregano daily, ideally as drops under the tongue, five to ten drops three or more times daily. Also consume a spice oil mix of wild oregano and sage oils, along with cumin and cinnamon oils , two or three times daily. As well, rub the oil all around the involved part of the lung area/rib cage as often as needed.

Optional

Fatty cod or sockeye salmon oil as a source of naturally occurring vitamin A, tablespoon daily or six to eight capsules daily, along with whole food, natural-source vitamin C from wild camu camu and acerola: two capsules twice daily.

Emphysema

While regarded as incurable by the medical profession, wild oregano offers great powers in aiding and reversing this condition. It is effective, because it combines antiseptic, anti-fungal, and antioxidative powers to help reverse the degenerative elements of this devastating condition. In many cases emphysema is related to mold infection deep within the lung tissues. Oil of wild oregano readily purges such molds from this organ, allowing the lung tissue to regenerate, leading to much improvement in this disease.

Treatment protocol

Take the oil of wild oregano, five to 10 drops under the tongue as often as necessary. As well, consume the aromatic essence or juice of wild oregano, a half ounce once or twice daily.

Optional

Take the fatty cod or sockeye salmon oil as source of truly whole food vitamin A, three capsules twice daily or two teaspoons daily. Consume also the whole food, non-synthetic vitamin pack complex containing whole food B complex, along with vitamins A, C, and E, one packet daily.

Tinnitus and Meniere's disease

This condition is related to a variety of causes, including viral infection and fungal infestation, the latter being caused mainly by molds. The molds infect the sinuses, disrupting the barometric pressure and leading to these conditions. As well, heavy metal poisoning can lead to these conditions. Another factor is a deficiency of nutrients, particularly vitamin A, vitamin C, and riboflavin.

Treatment protocol

Take the oil of wild oregano as drops under the tongue, five drops multiple times daily until all symptoms are eliminated. Also, rub the oil topically, as needed.

Optional

Consume also the whole food, non-synthetic vitamin pack complex containing whole food B complex, along with vitamins A, C, and E, one packet daily.

Chapter Six

Intestinal and Digestive Disorders

While the focus has been on respiratory disorders, incredibly, oil of wild oregano is equally valuable for digestive complaints. Virtually all digestive disorders respond positively to its immense therapeutic powers.

Irritable bowel syndrome/colitis

All forms of colitis, including irritable bowel syndrome and its related condition, spastic colitis, are readily reversible through oil of wild oregano therapy. The same is true of leaky gut syndrome, also fully purged through this potent treatment. The oil and the whole, crude herb are highly active in reversing all types of colitis, helping to purge all inflammatory reactions along the colonic mucosa.

Treatment protocol

Take the oil of wild oregano daily, five to ten drops two or three times daily, along with the whole, crude herbal complex, two capsules twice daily.

Optional

Digestive enzyme complex combined with spice concentrates, two or more capsules with each meal.

Ulcerative colitis

It seems that nothing, medically, can adequately treat this condition. Yet, once again, oil of wild oregano comes to the rescue, quickly obliterating it. For tough conditions the wild oregano essence is also a necessary therapy, working synergistically with the oil. Make no mistake in all cases of this condition if the oil and its associated whole food supplements are used aggressively, the condition will be reversed.

Treatment protocol

Take the oil of wild oregano, as drops under the tongue, five to ten drops two to four times daily. Also, consume the essence or juice of wild oregano, two or more tablespoons twice daily.

Optional

Digestive enzyme complex combined with spice concentrates, two or more capsules with each meal.

Crohn's disease

Though a most serious one this condition is largely reversible, which will shock many of those in the medical field. This is because the condition is directly related to infection. A novel kind of yeast is implicated, *Candida tropicalis*, along with the fungus-like microbe, *Mycobacterium tuberculosis*. It is a slow-growing form of TB that is involved. The pathogen infects the lower small intestine, possibly a consequence of the toxicity of standard immunizations. Regardless, all such pathogens are fully purged by oil of oregano therapy.

Treatment protocol

Take the oil of wild oregano daily, ideally as drops under the tongue, ten or more drops under the tongue three times daily, along with the juice or essence of wild oregano, one or more ounces twice daily. If using gel caps, take two twice daily.

Optional

Digestive enzyme complex combined with spice concentrates, two capsules with each meal.

Excessive gas

This is usually caused by the overgrowth of noxious pathogens within the intestinal canal, typically bacteria and/or fungi. Candida yeast is a major perpetrator of excessive gas formation. As well, food intolerance may lead to this, including an intolerance to gluten-containing grains. Another major perpetrator is excessive sugar consumption, which fed to yeast, causing bloating and gas production. Regarding any overgrowth of noxious organisms all such pathogens are readily eliminated through wild oregano therapy.

Treatment protocol

Take the oil of wild oregano daily as drops under the tongue or in juice/water, three to five drops twice daily. Also consume the whole, crude herbal complex with *Rhus coriaria*, two capsules twice daily.

Optional

Digestive enzyme complex combined with spice concentrates, two with each meal, along with a high-quality probiotic complex.

Halitosis

In halitosis or foul breath there may be disease of the teeth and gums, or there may be a disorder within the stomach and/or intestines. Often, the odor is caused by noxious bacteria, which overgrow in these regions. It may also be a sign of liver toxicity. Yet another fact is bacterial infection of the gums and teeth sockets. Wild oregano oil destroys the toxic, noxious bacteria, which cause this condition.

Treatment protocol

Take the oil of wild oregano drops under the tongue or in juice/water, five drops two or three times daily. If there is dental disease, use the oil as a dentifrice, also using the wild oregano/sage oil-based toothpaste along with its associated mouthwash, or ad sage and oregano oil to your toothpaste. Make sure your toothpaste is natural with no harmful chemicals or additives. Consult your local health food store.

Intestinal bloating

This condition is commonly caused by infestation of the gut by either fungi, that is yeasts, or parasites. Such bloating may also be a consequence of maldigestion from insufficient production of digestive enzymes. Another cause is food intolerance, particularly to wheat and dairy. As well, the regular or excessive consumption of refined sugar is a major factor. Such sugar feeds yeasts, leading to the symptoms.

Treatment protocol

Take the oil of wild oregano daily as drops under the tongue or in juice/water, five or more drops twice daily. Also consume the whole, crude herbal complex with *Rhus coriaria*, two capsules twice daily. Additionally, eliminate the intake of wheat and refined sugars.

Optional

Digestive enzyme complex combined with spice concentrates, two with each meal.

Giardia infection

A single-celled protozoal parasite, giardia mainly infects the lower stomach and upper small intestine, particularly the duodenum. Here, it causes much corruption, including excessive gas, bloating, inflammation, and food intolerance. Yet, the pathogen can readily be purged, in essence, burned out through oil of wild oregano therapy.

Treatment protocol

Take the oil of wild oregano, ideally as drops under the tongue, 10 to 20 drops three times daily or as gel caps, two or three twice daily, along with the whole, crude herbal complex, two capsules twice daily.

Esophagitis

For most people it would be hard to believe that such a condition involving irritation of the highly sensitive esophagus could benefit from a hot spice oil. Yet, it certainly does, and this is because the irritation is caused almost exclusively by infection. In one study it was found that up to 100 noxious bacteria can infect this organ, while yeasts and fungi may also be involved.

Treatment protocol

Take the oil of wild oregano, ideally as drops under the tongue, five drops two or three times daily, along with the whole crude herbal complex with *Rhus coriaria*, two capsules twice daily. If using gel caps, take one twice daily.

GERD/H. pylori

It has been stated that wild oregano is invaluable for digestive disorders. This is nowhere truer than in regard to H. pylori infection, the primary cause of gastroesophageal reflux, commonly known as GERD. This condition is synonymous with heartburn and/or upset stomach. In most instances, when such symptoms are chronic, infection of the stomach wall by H. pylori is the key factor. Oil of wild oregano obliterates this germ, while its efficacy is often enhanced by the simultaneous intake of the multiple spice oil capsules.

Treatment protocol

Take the oil of wild oregano daily, ideally as drops under the tongue, five to ten drops three times, or if taking gel caps two capsules twice daily. The whole crude herb with *Rhus coriaria* should also be consumed, three capsules twice daily.

Optional

Digestive enzyme complex combined with spice concentrates, two with each meal.

Gastritis

This condition may be caused by H. pylori, but there are other factors, like the excessive intake of alcohol and/or refined sugar. Regardless of the cause oil of wild oregano is a highly effective therapy, although its efficacy is enhanced by the ingestion of the whole, crude herbal complex with *Rhus coriaria*.

Treatment protocol

Take oil of wild oregano, three to five drops under the tongue twice daily, along with the whole crude herbal complex with *Rhus coriaria*, two capsules or more twice daily.

Optional

Digestive enzyme complex combined with spice concentrates, two with each meal.

Diarrhea

In most cases diarrhea is caused by infection of the intestinal wall, usually by bacteria, although viruses and the yeast are also perpetrators. Regardless of the cause the intake of oil of wild oregano, ideally as drops under the tongue, is an efficient, reliable therapy. Yet another effective therapy is raw honey, for instance, wild oregano honey.

Treatment protocol

Take the oil of wild oregano daily, as drops under the tongue, five drops as often as necessary to eliminate the symptoms. As well, consume raw, medicinal honey, for instance, manuka or wild oregano honey, two tablespoons two or more times daily. In extreme cases increase the dose to as much as four tablespoons three times daily, while mixing in additional oil of wild oregano.

Optional

probiotic complex, teaspoon first thing in the morning and also at bedtime in warm water.

Food poisoning

This is similar to diarrhea in the fact that this is the predominant symptom. Yet, food poisoning can also lead fever, chills, prostration, aches, and vomiting. With diarrhea and vomiting there is much loss of fluids and electrolytes. This is a disaster, which can readily lead to dehydration and hospitalization, even premature death.

Treatment protocol

Take the oil of wild oregano daily, as drops under the tongue, five to 10 drops five or more times daily, while also consuming the probiotic complex, tsp. first thing in the morning and also at bedtime in warm water.

Optional

For extreme cases it is advisable to also consume the wild oregano essence, a tablespoon multiple times daily, along with a wild-type honey, like wild oregano and/or thistle honey, two tablespoons multiple times daily. The honey halts fluid loss, while also providing much-needed nutrients, including potassium, in a form that can be readily absorbed.

C. difficle and E. coli

Make no mistake infections by these agents are no challenge to the powers of oil of wild oregano. No matter how extreme the case, rapidly, the oil, taken as drops under the tongue, rapidly purges such pathogens from the body. Treatment is greatly aided by the simultaneous intake of the juice of wild oregano, a high-quality, vigorously implanting probiotic, and wild-source, raw honey.

Treatment protocol

Take the oil of wild oregano under the tongue, five or more drops multiple times daily until the condition is resolved. Consume as well a whole food, high-implantation probiotic, a teaspoon in warm water at bedtime.

Optional

Consume also the juice of wild oregano, tablespoon twice daily, along with wild, raw honey, two tablespoons twice daily.

Appendicitis

While this is a medical emergency, still, the wild oregano oil, edible type, daily use, can be consumed. Though typically caused by bacteria appendicitis may also be induced by tapeworm infestation, with the fish tapeworm being the main perpetrator. In such a case oil of oregano is far superior to surgical treatment. The key is to use it as often as possible, while also applying it topically on the shins, bottoms of the feet, and also up and down the spine. If applied to the abdomen, this should be done with the utmost caution, gently.

Treatment protocol

Take the daily use, edible oil of wild oregano daily, ideally as drops under the tongue, 20 or more drops multiple times daily until the abdominal pain and various symptoms are eliminated. Also, rub the oil on the bottoms of the feet and up and down the shins as well as up and down the spine. As well, consume the juice or essence of wild oregano, two tablespoons several times daily.

Diverticulitis

In this condition infection predominates, although it can be aggravated by food intolerance and wrong diet. Diverticulitis is an infection of pockets or invaginations within the colonic wall. This is why oil of wild oregano is the most effective therapy for this condition known. It simply roots out all such infection, purging this syndrome.

Treatment protocol

Take the oil of wild oregano daily, ideally as drops under the tongue, five drops three or more times daily, while also consuming the juice/essence of wild oregano, one tablespoon two or three times daily. As a digestive aid consume also the whole, crude herb complex, two capsules twice daily.

Optional

Digestive enzyme complex combined with spice concentrates, two with each meal, along with the probiotic complex, half teaspoon at night in warm water, raw honey is also invaluable, two tablespoons twice daily.

Amebic infection (amebic dysentery)

In amebic dysentery there is infestation of the ameba in the lower colon. As well, the infection may spread to the liver as well as potentially the brain. While this is a medical emergency, even so, the wild oregano must be used, as it is exceedingly effective.

Treatment protocol

Take the oil of wild oregano daily, ideally as drops under the tongue, five to ten drops multiple times daily. If using the gel caps, take two or more three times daily. As well, consume the juice or essence of wild oregano, two tablespoons two or three times daily. Take also the probiotic complex, tsp. at night in warm water.

Cryptosporidium

Like giardia, this is an infection of the upper part of the small intestine, although the pathogen may also reside in lower parts and even the colon. A water-borne illness it causes much intestinal and digestive distress and, thus, the responsible pathogen must be vigorously eliminated.

Treatment protocol

Take the oil of wild oregano daily, ideally as drops under the tongue, 10 drops three times daily, along with the whole food, crude herbal complex, three capsules twice daily.

Optional

probiotic supplement, tsp. in warm water at bedtime and also first thing in the a.m.

Pinworms

In this condition tiny thread-like worms attack the intestinal canal, mainly in children. The worms live primarily in the rectal area and/or lower colon, where they cause intense itching, particularly at night. In fact, persistent anal itching in children is a categorical sign of pinworm infestation. Oil of wild oregano readily destroys such worms, although its efficacy is aided by the simultaneous intake of black seed oil and also oil of fennel in extra virgin olive oil.

Treatment protocol

Take the oil of wild oregano daily, ideally as drops under the tongue, three or more drops three times daily or as gel caps, one twice daily. Rub the oil on the lower spine and all over the buttocks being careful of the genitals. Consume also black seed oil, one teaspoon twice daily or as gel caps with fennel and cumin, one or two twice daily.

Optional

probiotic supplement, teaspoon in warm water at bedtime and wild, raw greens flushing agent, 2 dropperfuls twice daily.

Chapter Seven

Kidneys, Bladder, and More

Wild oregano is the most optimal, highly versatile therapeutic substance for virtually all bladder and kidney disorders known. It is also invaluable for disorders of the genital region. No other natural medicine can compare, as it directly attacks and purges the primary cause, which is infection. Plus, there is no concern of toxicity in the event of serious kidney disorders, particularly if it is used in reasonable amounts, like a few to several drops twice daily. Furthermore, in the event of serious kidney disease the whole, crude herbal complex with *Rhus coriaria* is a most ideal supplement, as it is completely non-toxic, while, in fact, aiding in reversing toxicity, including chronic kidney damage.

Prostatitis

In prostatitis, commonly, infection is the root cause. The 'itis' indicates inflammation. In one study conducted by Long Island University oil of wild oregano was even found to purge the most noxious cause of prostatic inflammation, cancer cells. All forms of prostatitis respond to the regular, daily intake of the oil. Another anti-prostatitis herb is *Rhus coriaria*, which is also a urinary antiseptic found in the whole, crude herbal complex.

Treatment protocol

Take the oil of wild oregano, ideally as drops under the tongue, five or more drops two or three times daily. As well, take the whole food wild oregano complex with the prostate-cleansing *Rhus coriaria*, two capsules twice daily.

Kidney/bladder stones

It has long been known that urinary stones are associated with chronic infection, notably by yeasts and bacteria. While oil of wild oregano purges these invaders it has also been found to directly act against stones, dissolving them. The urinary antiseptic, *Rhus coriaria*, also has this action.

Treatment protocol

Take the oil of wild oregano daily, ideally as drops under the tongue, 10 to 20 drops three times daily, along with the whole, crude herbal complex with *Rhus coriaria*, two or more capsules twice daily. If using the gel caps take two or three twice daily. In extreme cases double the dose and/or frequency.

Kidney infection

Kidney infections, known as pyelonephritis, are potential medical emergencies and must, thus, be treated aggressively. This is in order to prevent damage to this critical organ system. In some cases, the damage can be so severe that the kidneys fail, leading to dialysis and even death.

Treatment protocol

Take the oil of wild oregano, ideally as drops under the tongue, 10 to 20 or more drops three to five times daily. If taking the gel caps take two or three twice daily. Also, take the whole, crude herbal complex, three capsules three times.

Bladder infection and/or interstitial cystitis

Bladder infection is a highly common condition caused by various pathogens, including E. coli and candida yeast. While it is little realized interstitial cystitis is also a germ- related condition, the main perpetrators being various species of candida and other related invasive fungi.

Treatment protocol

Take the oil of wild oregano daily, as drops under the tongue, 10 to 20 drops three times daily, along with the whole, crude herbal complex, two capsules twice daily. For interstitial cystitis the dosage must be even more extreme, 30 drops four times daily, along with the whole crude herbal complex, three capsules twice daily. With such high doses there is a need to take probiotics, ideally the complex, a teaspoon in warm water at bedtime.

Genital warts

What a plague it is, warts attacking the genitals, including in females the cervix. Cervical warts are a major cause of cancer of this organ. In all instances wild oregano oil is the key purging agent, effective taken as sublingual drops. It may also be applied topically but in a much-diluted form, as it will cause a significant burning sensation in the genitals.

Treatment protocol

Take the oil of wild oregano daily as drops under the tongue, 20 drops four or more times daily. Also, apply topically in a diluted form, about 10:1 dilution with coconut oil or extra virgin olive oil.

Optional

Whole food, unprocessed bee propolis-wild oregano oil emulsion, 20 or more drops twice daily.

Genital herpes

In this plague of all plagues oil of wild oregano is a lifesaver. This is because it is fully capable of systematically purging this virus. To do so it must be taken in high doses, like 20 to 40 drops multiple times daily. There a number of case histories demonstrating the efficacy of this treatment, proven cases of total remission and, in fact, in many cases eradication of the disease. It has been found that the oil is greatly potentiated by the simultaneous intake of emulsified bee propolis in a wild oregano oil base.

Treatment protocol

Take the super-strength oil of wild oregano daily, as drops under the tongue, 20 or more drops four times daily. If taking gel caps, take three capsules four or five times daily. Note: for genital herpes the ideal type of oil of oregano to use is the ultra-formula with 84%-plus carvacrol.

Optional

Consume also the whole food, raw propolis emulsion in extra virgin olive oil and wild oregano oil, 40 drops two or three times daily, along with whole food, CO2-extracted cannabis plus wild CO2-extracted oregano, 40 drops twice daily.

Infertility

This condition is commonly caused by chronic infection in the genital organs, notably by the yeast, *Candida albicans*. Other infectious agents which can disrupt fertility include gonococcus, herpes, chlamydia, trichomonas, and spirochetal

organisms. In all such cases oil of wild oregano is a godsend, and by destroying such invasive pathogens it can rapidly restore fertility. A number of nutritional deficiencies are associated with infertility, notably a lack of vitamin A and the B complex. As well, vitamin E deficiency is associated with fertility disorders. Thus, it is often necessary to replenish these nutrients through whole food, non- synthetic sources, including whole food supplements. As well, the thyroid gland

and adrenal glands play a major role in enhancing fertility. Thus, these glands must be supported to achieve optimal results. Additionally, certain superfoods aid in assisting fertility regeneration, including high-quality maca, royal jelly, and ashwagandha.

Treatment protocol

Take the oil of wild oregano daily, five to ten drops two or more times daily. Also, for known infection of the genital or pelvic region, rub the oil on the pit of the low back and over the sacrum. Consume also the whole food, non-synthetic vitamin pack complex containing whole food B complex, along with vitamins A, C, and E, one packet daily.

Optional

Consume also the whole food wild, remote-source sockeye salmon oil, three capsules twice daily, along with the thyroid-adrenal-supporting activating herbal, royal jelly, and kelp complex, two capsules twice daily. Additionally, consume an ashwagandha-royal jelly combination, one or two capsules twice daily as well as a raw, whole food purple maca concentrate as drops under the tongue, 40 drops twice daily.

Endometriosis

In this condition, like countless others, there is infestation in the female genital organs and also in the pelvic region, the primary culprit being *Candida albicans*. This leads to significant inflammation, causing much distress during menses and also pelvic pain. Another possible cause is sexual intercourse during menses, which causes a backflush of menstrual fluid into the fallopian tubes. Nutritional deficiency plays a role, notably a deficit of B complex and vitamin A. Endometriosis may also be related to insufficient function of the adrenal glands as well as the ovaries and thyroid themselves.

Treatment protocol

Take the oil of wild oregano daily, five drops three times daily or as gel caps, one three times daily. As well, consume the juice or essence of wild oregano, a tablespoon once or twice daily. Take also the whole food, full complex probiotic, , a teaspoon in warm water at bedtime.

Optional

Consume a whole food, non-synthetic vitamin complex as a packet of nine capsules, including fatty sockeye salmon oil, sunflower vitamin E, and whole food B complex caps: one packet daily, along with capsules of royal jelly with wild rosemary and sage, two caps twice daily.

Ovarian cysts

With this condition, once again, infestation of the pelvis by *Candida albicans* plays a predominant role. Yet another factor is weakness or insufficiency in the thyroid and adrenal glands, which, to a degree, may be caused by nutritional deficiency. The excess consumption of caffeine and refined sugar are additional causative factors. The cysts may also be a sign of vitamin E deficiency, along with a deficit of vitamin A, much needed for the regeneration of ovarian tissue.

Treatment protocol

Take the oil of wild oregano, five drops under the tongue twice daily. Also, rub the oil all about the lower pelvis near the area of the ovaries. Additionally, take whole food vitamins, including sunflower vitamin E and food-based B complex nutrients, one packet of ten capsules daily. Avoid the intake of refined sugar, aspartame, and caffeine.

Optional

Take capsules of royal jelly with wild rosemary and sage, two caps twice daily as well as a whole food thyroid-supporting complex with tyrosine, rosemary, and kelp, one capsule twice daily.

PMS

In this condition there is, surely, an imbalance in hormone production. Yet, typically, there is also an overgrowth of candida yeast, the pathogen being encouraged to invade as a result of the hormone imbalance. This is why the intake of refined sugar is so devastating, leading to PMS and, often, severe cramping. By destroying the candida, wild oregano oil eases and even reverses this condition. Its efficacy is aided by the simultaneous intake of royal jelly and kelp, which aid in balancing ovarian function. Vitamins A and E, as well as the B complex, also aid in calming PMS symptoms.

Treatment protocol

Take oil of wild oregano, ideally just before the period, five drops two or three times daily. As well, take a royal jelly, kelp, and fenugreek combination, two capsules twice daily and as a preventive therapy, two caps daily.

Optional

Consume also the whole food, non-synthetic vitamin pack complex containing whole food B complex, along with vitamins A, C, and E, one packet daily.

Depression

Regarded as a chemical imbalance, even a hormonal disorder, depression may not be so mysterious after all. In many cases it is caused at least in part by chronic infection. This is why, commonly, oil of wild oregano therapy is successful. It is rarely emphasized how significant the role of infection is in mental disorders, including anxiety-neurosis, depression, and schizophrenia. In addition to the oil, the aromatic essence or juice of wild oregano is rich in molecular oxygen and, thus, may help combat this condition. As well, whole food, cannabis is a most potent therapeutic agent, especially the type complexed with wild oregano.

Treatment protocol

Take the oil of wild oregano, five drops under the tongue twice daily or as gel caps, one twice daily. As well, consume the juice of wild oregano, one tablespoon twice daily.

Optional

Consume also the whole food, non-synthetic vitamin complex containing whole food B complex, along with vitamins A, C, and E, one packet daily. Additionally, consume the raw, whole food cannabis-hemp extract complexed with wild, whole food CO2-extracted oregano, five or more drops twice daily.

Chapter Eight

The Outer Body, Skin, Mouth, and More

The oral cavity, skin, and mucous membranes greatly benefit from the use of oil of wild oregano and its associated supplements. There is often need for other supplemental support such as the intake of whole food B complex, appropriate amounts of protein, natural-source vitamin C, and whole food, unprocessed vitamin A. Let us review the multiplicity of uses of oil of wild oregano for conditions in these regions.

Scrapes, cuts, and abrasions

In such conditions, clearly, what is needed is a generalized antiseptic, which is precisely the nature of the oil of wild oregano. It is ideal, as it not only sterilizes the wound but also speeds healing, preventing scarring, while also easing pain.

Treatment protocol

Apply the oil to the area once or twice daily or as needed. If the cut or abrasion is large also apply raw honey, cover with gauze. Seek medical attention if necessary.

Bruises

Nothing can positively reverse bruises as well as oil of wild oregano. It mobilizes the bruise matter, causing it to be absorbed into the lymphatic system. The oil also eliminates any bruise-associated swelling and pain. Even so, bruises are a sign of certain deficiencies, notably a deficit of vitamin C and also vitamin K.

Treatment protocol

If possible, immediately treat the bruised area. Vigorously rub the oil of oregano over the bruise site until any swelling and/or the bruise is resolved.

Optional

Take a whole food vitamin C complex free of all corn-based, GMO-tainted ascorbic acid, one capsule twice daily.

Gum disease

Gum disease, or pyorrhea, is a consequence of a combination of nutritional deficiencies and infection. Refined sugar is a major perpetrator in inducing degeneration of this tissue. Another major factor in gum breakdown is the consumption of alcohol. Regardless, oil of wild oregano reverses this condition, especially if it is routinely applied topically.

Treatment protocol

Take the oil of wild oregano as drops under the tongue, three to five drops twice daily. Also, use the oil as a dentifrice and apply to gum area once or twice daily. Use the specialized additive- and glycerin-free toothpaste with oils of wild oregano oil and sage plus clove oil, for supporting healthy gums and teeth, while avoiding the use of all toothpastes with chemical additives and fluoride. In particular, glycerin is highly damaging to gum tissue, causing them to be weak and flabby, which more readily allows bacterial invasion.

Optional

A specialized dental oil complex is also advisable. Use a combination of oils of wild oregano, clove, and cinnamon, which is also ideal for applying topically. Consult your health food store for the best dental products.

Toothache

Toothache is nearly always caused by a severe infection, usually an abscess. The abscess is caused by noxious bacteria, notably anaerobes. Far superior to antibiotics oil of oregano is a potent treatment for this condition. Since it is a germicide, it destroys all bacterial types responsible for this ailment. It also eases pain and inflammation.

Treatment protocol

Take the oil of wild oregano, five drops under the tongue multiple times daily. Also apply the oil topically as often as necessary. Another option is to apply topically the specialized dental oil complex consisting of oils of wild oregano plus cinnamon and clove oils once again, for supporting healthy teeth and gums.

Leukoplakia

While it is not commonly realized, this condition manifested by oral lesions is largely a consequence of fungal infestation, notably by the yeast, *Candida albicans* and similar fungal invaders. This is why oil of wild oregano is the most effective therapy known for this condition.

Treatment protocol

Take the oil of wild oregano, five drops under the tongue two or more times daily. Also, repeatedly apply the oil, topically.

Optional

Whole food fatty cod or sockeye salmon oil rich in naturally occurring vitamins A and D plus astaxanthin, two or more capsules twice daily.

Boils and abscesses

With boils and abscesses, obviously, infection is the cause. While most doctors treat these as bacterial infections in some cases candida may be involved. In all such lesions wild oregano oil is the most effective treatment, more potent and thorough in its powers than antibiotics. Plus, the oil kills both bacteria and yeasts, which antibiotics cannot achieve.

Treatment protocol

Take the oil of wild oregano, five drops under the tongue a few times daily. Also, apply the oil topically. As well, use the multiple spice oil-based emulsified spray, applying topically. Or spray it into cotton and apply for constant contact.

Cold sores

For cold sores oil of wild oregano is ideal, because it can not only be applied topically but also taken internally. The internal therapy offers both preventive and curative actions. Yet another effective anti-cold sore and, thus, antiherpetic therapy is bee propolis, especially the naturally emulsified form in a wild oregano oil base. This, too, can be applied topically and taken internally.

Treatment protocol

Take the oil of wild oregano, ideally as drops under the tongue, three to five drops two or three times daily. Also, apply the oil topically as often as needed. As an option also take the emulsified propolis extract (alcohol- free), five to 10 drops once or twice daily, also applying topically.

Acne

For acne of all types nothing is superior to oil of wild oregano. It is versatile, as it can be taken internally and also applied topically. It simply burns out the acne, never again to return.

Nutritional deficiencies also play a role in this condition. Key nutrients that are deficient include vitamins A, D, and E, along with vitamin C and the B complex. In addition, commonly, there is a deficit in essential fatty acids. Wrong diet plays a significant role, with deep fried food, refined sugar, and refined vegetable oils greatly aggravating the condition.

Treatment protocol

Take the oil of wild oregano, five or more drops under the tongue two to four times daily. Also, apply the oil topically as often as necessary. Or using cotton simply dab it on constantly. To correct the nutritional deficiencies the whole food, chemical-free, and additive-free vitamin pack should be consumed, one packet daily, along with whole food essential fatty acids, like hemp seed oil or sacha inchi oil, two tablespoons daily. As well, whole food non-soy-based vitamin E can be consumed and also used on the face topically.

Seborrhea

This condition is caused by a combination of infestation, usually by fungi/yeasts, and nutritional deficiency. Destructive dietary practices are also a key factor, notably the intake of refined sugar, corn syrup, and refined vegetable oils. Key deficient nutrients include riboflavin, vitamin A, vitamin D, essential fatty acids, zinc, and pyridoxine.

Treatment protocol

Take oil of wild oregano, five drops under the tongue twice daily, also applying it topically.

Optional

Take a truly whole food source of vitamins as a pack complex, one or two packets daily, along with a whole food, additive free B complex powder, two or more tablespoons daily. As well, raw chaga is highly potent against this condition, especially as sublingual drops in a base of wild oil of oregano, cinnamon oil, and clove bud oil.

Eczema

Typically, a stubborn condition this is a consequence of a combination of destructive dietary practices, immune system corruptions, food intolerance, infection, and nutritional deficiency. Striking children aggressively, here, it may also be the result of the toxicity of immunizations. Such immunizations destabilize the immune system, resulting in reactive eczema and dermatitis. Additionally, eczema is related to a deficiency of skin tissue regenerative, factors, including vitamins A and E, vitamin D, the B complex, essential fatty acids, and omega 3 fatty acids. In addition to oregano wild chaga helps reverse this condition.

Treatment protocol

Take the oil of wild oregano, as drops under the tongue, 5 to 10 drops three times daily, along with the whole, crude herbal complex, two capsules twice daily. As well, consume a complex of vitamins A and D plus 33 omega 3s as fatty, wild sockeye salmon oil, one or two teaspoons daily, along with essential fatty acids in the form of sacha inchi oil, one tablespoon daily.

Optional

Raw chaga is highly potent against this condition, especially as sublingual drops in a base of wild oil of oregano, cinnamon oil, and clove bud oil—use topically and also take internally, 20 or more drops twice daily.

Rosacea

It was, once again, through *The Cure is in the Cupboard* that the most effective treatment for rosacea was discovered. It is simply the topical and internal use of the oil of wild oregano. The condition is caused largely by infestation of the sebaceous glands of the face by the demodex mite, although there is a correlation with infection of the stomach wall by H. pylori. Regardless, wild oregano oil is active against both these infections, which explains its high degree of efficacy against all forms of rosacea.

Treatment protocol

Take the oil of wild oregano as drops under the tongue, five to 10 drops twice daily. For stubborn conditions take 10 to 20 drops three times daily. Additionally, apply the oil topically repeatedly on the rosacea lesions; natural heat sensation is normal.

Optional

Apply a wild oregano and lavender oil-based cream in a Canadian balsam-raw honey base twice daily. Consume fatty cod or sockeye salmon oil rich in naturally occurring vitamins A and D, three capsules twice daily.

Decubitus ulcers (bed sores)

No doubt, wild oil of oregano is the primary therapeutic agent for all open, non-healing wounds, including all types of skin ulcerations. Here, it is most efficacious when combined with wild, raw honey such as wild oregano or wild thistle honeys. The manuka type is another option. Additionally, nutritional deficiencies exist to the extreme, with deficits of vitamins A and D, along with vitamin C and the B complex, being routine.

Treatment protocol

Take the oil of wild oregano, five to 10 drops under the tongue three times daily. Also, apply the oil combined with raw honey, about five drops per tablespoon and cover, changing once or twice daily. The oregano oil will burn-out and destroy any infection, regardless of the pathogen.

Optional

Consume also the whole food, non-synthetic vitamin pack complex containing whole food B complex, along with vitamins A, C, and E, one packet daily.

Moles

There can be no doubt about it, moles can be cleansed from the body. Some are unsightly, others seemingly of no issue, while still others can be pre-cancerous. Regardless, they can all be efficiently purged through wild oregano oil therapy: without surgery or chemical application.

Refined sugar may increase the number of moles and also cause existing ones to grow in size. So does refined vegetable oil, which is, in fact, a carcinogen. Deep fried food is also carcinogenic, its consumption putting people with moles at a higher risk of cancerous degeneration. Oregano oil's antioxidant powers also aid in combating moles and their potential degeneration into skin cancer.

Treatment protocol

Take oil of wild oregano, five or more drops under the tongue twice daily. Also, apply the oil to the involved region(s) as often as possible. For continuous contact saturate or cotton and apply, changing once or twice daily.

Skin cancer

A major plague of modern humanity, particularly for light- skinned, Western people, the fact that this can be treated with natural medicines is little known. Typically, skin cancer is treated surgically. Yet, this poses a dilemma, as the cancer can return or resurface in other areas. A superior therapy is the use of wild oregano oil, both internally and topically. In fact, it is highly effective in this regard for all this disease's manifestations, including squamous cell, basal cell, and melanoma. As well, because of its potent antioxidant powers it both destroys skin cancer and, if taken regularly, prevents its development.

Treatment protocol

Take the oil of wild oregano, ideally as drops under the tongue, five to ten drops or more two or three times daily. Also, rub it on repeatedly topically where needed. The emulsified bee propolis may also be applied for synergetic effects.

Age spots and precancerous lesions

There are a number of skin lesions that are regarded as precancerous, for instance, senile keratoses and moles, which are changing in appearance. There are also those associated with age-related degeneration, for instance, the typical age or liver spots. All such lesions can be routinely treated with the oil of oregano as a potent antioxidant and cancer-prevention agent.

Treatment protocol

Take oil of wild oregano, above five drops twice daily, while also vigorously rubbing the oil two or more times daily on any suspect lesions. For prolonged contact saturate a bit of cotton and paper tape onto the lesion/age spot site.

Warts

For warts there are relatively few natural medicines known to aggressively eliminate them. The milky sap of milk weed is somewhat effective, as is the same type of sap from dandelions. It is much easier, though, to use the oil of wild oregano, ideally in a super-strength form or the novel ultra-formulation. Through aggressive internal intake plus saturation of the involved sites the warts can be readily purged.

Treatment protocol

Take the oil of wild oregano, 20 or more drops under the tongue or in juice/water twice or more daily. As well, saturate any involved area with the oil, and for constant contact keep the oil applied with saturated cotton. A 24-hour application is ideal for rapid elimination of the lesions. For stubborn conditions use the specialized wild oregano oil ultra-potent formula with 84%-plus carvacrol.

Paronychia

This condition is usually caused by candida infection of the fingernail beds, although staph may also be a factor. Regardless of the cause wild oregano is the answer, since through its germicidal powers the pathogens will be eliminated and, thus, the swelling and pain are resolved.

Treatment protocol

Take the oil of wild oregano, ideally as drops under the tongue, five to 10 drops three times daily. Also, saturate involved site(s) with the oil, a super-strength form being most effective for these lesions.

Shingles

Caused by an outbreak of the so-called chicken pox virus, a herpetic agent, shingles is highly resistant to all orthodox medical treatments. Even so, it readily succumbs to aggressive use of the wild oregano oil, a super-strength blend being the ideal therapeutic intervention. Another most potent therapy is wild, raw non-alcoholic propolis emulsion. Such a complex is highly anti-herpetic while also being a potent immune stimulant.

Treatment protocol

Take the oil of wild oregano as drops under the tongue, 10 or more drops multiple times daily. Also, apply the oil topically as often as needed until the condition is fully resolved.

Optional

For stubborn conditions also take emulsified wild propolis, that is the propolis-wild oregano oil complex, 20 drops under the tongue two or more times daily.

Ringworm

An irritating, itchy condition ringworm is caused by a skin fungus, resulting in annular, that is circular, types of lesions. Related to the same germ that causes athlete's foot, it is quickly eliminated by the aggressive use of oil of wild oregano, both topically and internally. The secret for rapid results is consistent contact, along with consumption internally.

Treatment protocol

Take the oil of wild oregano daily, 10 or more drops three times daily. Also, apply the oil repeatedly to the suspect lesion(s), rubbing in, if possible, vigorously. Or saturate cotton with the oil of wild oregano, ideally an extra-strength formula, and paper-tape on; change every 12 hours or keep on continuously.

Athlete's foot/jock itch

Athlete's foot and jock itch are caused by skin fungal organisms, known as dermatophytes. The organisms cause excoriation of the skin, along with much itching and irritation. Taken internally, oil of wild oregano is highly effective against these conditions. For athlete's foot it can also be apply topically, vigorously rubbed into the involved region(s). It should also be applied between the toes, where the fungus readily hides and invades. Moreover, it can be applied on the region and then a sock can be placed over it to create consistent contact. For jock itch topical application will lead to much burning of the testicles. Here, the oil must be diluted at least 10:1 with extra virgin olive oil before application.

Treatment protocol

Take the oil of wild oregano daily, ideally as drops under the tongue, about 10 to 20 drops two or three times daily. In some cases, as little as five drops twice daily will suffice. Diluted apply topically, as needed.

Optional

Take probiotic, teaspoon in warm water at bedtime.

Nail fungus

One of the most stubborn conditions known, nail fungus has a special attribute. Once it sets in it is seemingly incurable by the human immune system. Even medical treatments have proven virtually impotent at eradicating it. The condition is caused by the infectious agents, known as the dermatophytes, which under certain conditions thrive on human skin as well as keratin or nail tissue. This condition involves excess moisture and heat as well as a weakened immune system, excessive sugar consumption, and possibly localized injury.

Treatment protocol

For this stubborn condition take the oil of wild oregano, super-strength variety, in a high dose, about 40 drops under the tongue or in juice/water two or more times daily. In some cases, it may be necessary to take 80 drops twice daily. Clip the diseased nail(s) back as much as possible; vigorously rub the oil into the infested nail(s) once or twice daily. Take also probiotic, teaspoon in warm water at bedtime, as high-dose wild oregano therapy may act to reduce levels of the healthy bacteria. Note: for the eradication of toenail fungus the ideal type of oil of oregano to use is the ultra-formula with 84%-plus carvacrol. Such a density of carvacrol increases the potency power of the oil and increases the penetration of the nail bed.

Hives

For this condition wild oregano is the most optimal therapeutic agent known. The lesions of hives are largely a result of histamine production. The source of the histamine is either allergic intolerance or parasitic infestation. Commonly, giardia, as well as tapeworms and roundworms, cause this condition. As a potent antihistamine wild oregano largely reverses this it. This is particularly true of the drops, which can be taken under the tongue and also applied topically. Yet, the whole, crude herb is a dense source of quercetin, which helps combat hives and other allergic toxicities. Hives may also be a sign of adrenal exhaustion, so therapy aimed at this glandular system also aids in reversing it.

Treatment protocol

Take the oil of wild oregano under the tongue, five or more drops multiple times daily until all symptoms and signs are eliminated. Also, rub the oil topically, as needed.

Optional

For adrenal support take a whole food, undiluted royal jelly complex with wild sage and rosemary, two capsules two or more times daily.

Burns

Wild oregano oil is one of the most effective natural medicines for burns known. This is true of all degrees, first, second, and third. For optimal results wild, raw honey can also be used, either wild oregano or manuka honeys. Oil of wild oregano prevents any infection from burns, while also speeding healing; its intake and application also prevents blister formation and scarring. The same is true of raw honey, which is the most effective salve or ointment for burns known. The oregano oil and honey can be combined for optimal effect, about five drops or so per tablespoon.

Treatment protocol

Apply the oil of wild oregano to the burn site(s) as often as necessary. If the burns are extreme, if possible, mix the oil with raw, wild honey, for instance, wild oregano or manuka, and apply, covering with gauze. As well, consume the oil, five to 10 drops a few times daily. For burns covering a large percentage of the body it is necessary to support the adrenal glands; take a royal jelly supplement complexed with wild rosemary and sage, two or more capsules twice daily.

Optional

Oil of wild lavender in an extra virgin olive oil base and also the anti-inflammatory complex of bromelain and papain plus turmeric and ginger, the latter being taken in a dose of three capsules two or more times daily on an empty stomach.

Sunburn

Oil of wild oregano is highly effective against this condition. This may surprise many people, since it is such a burning hot oil. It is as if a homeopathic concept, like versus like, that is a hot spice oil on burned tissue. The oil shuts down the burn reaction, halting the inflammation. The addition of raw, wild honey often improves the results, especially in the event of third-degree burns. The sooner the oregano oil is applied the more quickly will be the induction of healing. As well, raw honey contains enzymes, which speed the healing of any damaged tissue.

Treatment protocol

Apply the oregano oil on the sunburn several times daily while also taking it under the tongue, about five drops four or five times daily. In severe burns a higher dose can be used, at least 10 drops under the tongue at a time. Apply the honey as a soothing agent in a thin layer to the more severe spots and cover gently with gauze repeating every 12 hours. Oregano oil can be mixed with the honey before applying, two to five drops per tablespoonful.

Optional

Apply true wild oil of lavender in an extra virgin olive oil base, as needed. Lavender oil speeds the healing of burns, eases pain, and aids in prevention of scarring.

Chapter Nine

Joints, Muscles, and Nerves

While it is little realized wild oregano has immense utility in combating disorders of the joints, muscles, and nervous system, while also combating related pain and inflammation. Once again, infection is a major factor behind these conditions. For instance, some 80% of all cases of arthritis are infectious in origin. The same is true of muscular pain syndromes such as fibromyalgia and polymyositis rheumatica. It makes sense that they are infectious. Otherwise, how could there be this degree of inflammation? Oregano oil is also anti-inflammatory and possesses significant pain-relieving powers, making it an ideal rubbing oil for muscular and skeletal disorders. No other substance possesses such broad-spectrum pain-relieving, germ-killing, and anti-inflammatory powers. In particular, the higher carvacrol types have exceptional power in this regard, particularly the novel, new 84% wild carvacrol type.

Muscular pain and/or fibromyalgia

While, certainly, injuries and strain patterns play a major role in muscular pain conditions, as well, so does infection.

It is such chronic infections which cause the inflammation that leads to the pain, for instance, infestation by parasites, candida, and/or the Lyme bacillus. Black mold exposure may also lead to much pain and inflammation. Other factors include structural imbalances, for instance, osteopathic lesions and also nutritional deficits, like a deficiency of the B complex and magnesium.

Treatment protocol

Take the oil of wild oregano, five to 10 drops twice daily, along with the whole, crude herbal complex, two or more capsules twice daily.

Optional

Consume also a whole food, non-synthetic vitamin pack complex containing whole food B complex, along with vitamins A, C, and E, one packet daily, along with 200 to 400 mg of chelated magnesium daily.

Joint and bone pain

For any type of joint or bone pain the intake of oregano oil is ideal. Then, too, it can also be applied topically. As well, the whole, crude herbal complex with *Rhus coriaria* is synergistic with the oil. Plus, it provides minerals and vitamin K, essential for joint and bone tissue repair. Vitamin C is also required for optimal health of the bones and joints, needed, in particular, for the formation of a specialized substance, known as ground substances, which is, essentially, intercellular cement. The only vitamin C worthy of consumption is either from food or as a supplement, whole food sources. Avoid synthetic ascorbic acid like the plague. Additionally, vitamins A, D, and K are essential for strong bones and healthy joint tissue.

Treatment protocol

Take the oil of wild oregano, five or more drops two or more times daily. Also, take the whole, crude herbal complex, two or more capsules twice daily. Note: for pain syndromes the ideal type of oil of oregano to use is the ultra-formula with 84%-plus carvacrol.

Optional

Consume also a whole food, non-synthetic vitamin pack complex containing whole food B complex, along with vitamins A, C, and E, one packet daily. For stubborn conditions osteopathic manipulative therapy may be necessary.

Shin splints

Shin splints most commonly occur in developing children or teens, who virtually outgrow the capacity of their connective tissues to keep pace. Here, inflammation occurs about the interosseous membrane between the tibia and fibula. In this regard, both topically and internally, the oil of wild oregano is invaluable, but so are the bone activating rubbing oil and the bone activating spice-based capsules.

Treatment protocol

Take the oil of wild oregano, two or three drops under the tongue once or twice daily or as gel caps one daily. As well, use the oil topically, scrubbing it vigorously into the involved regions. For difficult cases take the bone activating spice-based capsules with raw New Zealand cattle bone, while also rubbing on the bone activating rubbing oil.

Tendonitis and bursitis

In these conditions there is obvious inflammation, locally, in the joints and attached connective tissue. These structural

disorders respond exceedingly well to oil of wild oregano therapy. Once again, both topical and internal use is recommended. For effective relieve topical application is ideally multiple times daily.

Treatment protocol

Take the oil of wild oregano daily, five or more drops twice daily. As well, vigorously rub the oil into the involved tissues, repeating, as needed. For stubborn conditions osteopathic manipulative therapy may be necessary.

Optional

Consume a whole food, raw, crude turmeric complex with raw, organic cannabis extract, 20 drops twice daily or two gel caps twice daily.

Fractures

In Turkey, where oregano grows wild, the oil is commonly applied to severe injuries, including fractures. It was Turkish investigators who determined that oil of wild oregano was nearly half as effective as morphine in combating pain, finding it equally effective as non-steroidal anti-inflammatory agents. As well, it aids in inducing tissue healing, both of open wounds and the actual fractured bone itself. It may also be necessary to consume the bone- activating capsules, while also applying the rubbing oil, both of which dramatically enhance fracture healing.

Treatment protocol

Take the oil of wild oregano daily, five drops as often as necessary. Also, immediately after injury apply the oil to the involved region. Note: for pain syndromes the ideal type of oil of oregano to use is the ultra-formula with 84%-plus carvacrol.

Optional (but highly recommended)

Consume bone-activating capsules containing high-grade microcrystalline hydroxyapatite-rich raw bone from New Zealand cattle, along with wild rosemary, sage, and oregano, three or more capsules twice daily, while also using the bone-activating rubbing oil.

Spinal stiffness

A number of conditions are related to spinal stiffness, including Lyme disease, ankylosing spondylitis, tuberculosis, arthritis, intestinal parasitism, and spinal stenosis. In all such syndromes there is much inflammation. Even so, many of these diseases are directly connected to infection. In many cases the intake of wild oregano oil can ease the stiffness and rigidity. For extra power in reversing this the consumption of bromelain and papain is advised. Extracts of turmeric and ginger are also highly powerful in combating inflammatory disorders of the spine. As well, the topical application of the oil, as well as the bone-activating rubbing oil, is a highly effective therapy for both reducing the inflammatory reaction and, thus, increasing movement and flexibility within this organ.

Yet another valuable therapy is the intake of high-terpene, raw, CO2-extracted cannabis extracts, particularly the type complexed with wild oregano oil. In difficult conditions, therefore, it may be necessary to use a number of therapeutic agents, particularly in the event of infestation of the spinal column by pathogens, as occurs in Lyme and tuberculosis. Additionally, osteopathic manipulative therapy is an effective modality for enhancing mobility in the spinal column.

The stiffness may also be a sign of nutritional deficiency. Lacking nutrients include magnesium, phosphorus, zinc, copper, vitamin C, the B complex, and vitamins A, D, and K.

Treatment protocol

Take the oil of wild oregano, ideally as drops under the tongue, 10 or more drops twice daily. Also, rub the oil up and down the spine once or twice daily, and for difficult cases also apply the bone-activating rubbing oil. Additionally, take the whole food, unprocessed cannabis plus wild turmeric and ginger extract, two or more capsules twice daily. For stubborn conditions osteopathic manipulative therapy may be necessary. Note: for pain and inflammation syndromes the ideal type of oil of oregano to use is the ultra-formula with 84%-plus carvacrol.

Optional

Consume a whole food, raw, crude turmeric complex with raw, organic cannabis extract, 20 drops twice daily or two gel caps twice daily about two to three caps twice daily on an empty stomach. As well, take a whole food, non-synthetic vitamin pack complex containing whole food B complex, along with vitamins A, C, and E, one packet daily, along with 200 to 400 mg of chelated magnesium daily.

Dupertryn's contracture

In virtually all instances this syndrome is caused by infectious agents. Yet, in the medical system this cause is virtually never considered. Thus, the diagnosis and cure remain elusive. A septic tooth on the same side as the contracture. Yet another is Lyme spirochete invasion. As well, the contracture is associated with a deficiency of vitamin E.

Treatment protocol

Rub topically into the contracted area high-strength form of oil of wild oregano, either a super-strength formula or an ultra-high carvacrol formula, a dropperful multiple times daily. Rub the oil both about the obviously contracted area and also up and down the tendonous sheath on the fleshly part of the wrist all the way to the elbow. Also, take the oil internally, 10 or more drops two or three times daily. Consume whole

food vitamin E complex as sunflower seed oil vitamin E, one or two capsules twice daily.

Optional

Take an anti-inflammatory enzyme complex with uncoated, high-dose bromelain and papain: three capsules three times daily on an empty stomach and/or the whole food cannabis-turmeric complex, two caps twice daily.

Torticollis

Torticollis or wry neck is a rather rare condition listed in medicine as cause unknown.' Yet, in some cases it may be related to chronic infection of the spinal tissues or brain by viruses, parasites, and other pathogens. While oil of oregano is an effective therapy it is synergized with the simultaneous intake of the juice/essence, raw, unprocessed cannabis extract, and wild, raw turmeric extract. In the event of traumatic injury of the neck it may also be necessary to apply proper osteopathic technique.

Treatment protocol

Take the oil of wild oregano drops, 10 or more drops multiple times daily, along with the juice/essence, two tablespoons twice daily. As well, consume the cannabis-wild oregano complex, 10 or more drops twice daily or as gel caps, two twice daily.

Optional

Take wild, raw turmeric extract complex with ginger and/or a cannabis- turmeric combination, two capsules twice daily.

Bell's palsy

Bell's palsy is virtually always directly related to infection, the Lyme bacillus and various viruses being the main perpetrators. Another factor is direct trauma to the face, skull, or neck. Stress may also induce it, but it does so by suppressing the immune system, allowing the pathogens to invade the nerve sheath, in this case the cranial nerve known as the facial nerve. A deficiency of the B vitamin pantothenic acid may be related. Weak or exhausted adrenal glands increase the vulnerability for an attack of this condition.

Treatment protocol

Take the oil of wild oregano, five to 10 drops under the tongue multiple times daily, also rubbing the oil topically repeatedly. As well, consume the juice or essence of wild oregano, one or two tablespoons twice daily. Additionally, take a high-quality royal jelly supplement for supporting the adrenal glands, two capsules twice daily.

Optional

Consume a whole food cannabis plus wild turmeric extract, two capsules twice daily or as sublingual drops, 20 or more drops twice daily. As well, increase the consumption of pantothenic acid-rich foods such as whole, organic eggs, grass-fed meat, broccoli, spinach, brewer's yeast, organic liver/heart, rice bran, peanuts, and canned pumpkin.

Chronic hip pain/inflammation

A plague of modern society this eventually leads in many cases to artificial hip replacement surgery. In many cases such surgery can be prevented by aggressive use of wild oregano and associated supplements such as the bone activating capsules and rubbing oil. Wild turmeric also has much power, here, and its regular intake greatly reduces pain and inflammation in this joint.

Treatment protocol

Take the oil of wild oregano, five to 10 drops under the tongue two or more times daily. Also, consume the organic, natural, raw cannabis plus raw, wild turmeric complex, one or two capsules twice daily. Note: the ideal type of wild oregano oil to use for pain/inflammations syndromes is the ultra-potent 84%-plus carvacrol formula.

Optional

Consume also the whole food, non-synthetic vitamin pack complex containing whole food B complex, along with vitamins A, C, and E, one packet daily, along with a whole food, raw, crude turmeric complex with raw, organic cannabis extract, 20 drops twice daily or two gel caps twice daily. For stubborn conditions osteopathic manipulative therapy may be necessary.

Leg cramps

In this condition there is severe spasticity of the muscles, Largely due to nutritional deficiency the deficient nutrients include magnesium and the B complex. There is also a deficit of oxygen in the muscles, which is responsible. In some cases, leg cramps may be related to pathology such as tapeworm infestation or even infection of the brain by parasites. Regardless, oil of oregano, as well as the whole, crude herbal complex, is an effective therapy for sudden- onset leg or foot cramps. As an oxygen source the juice or essence can also be consumed.

Treatment protocol

Take the oil of wild oregano, five drops twice daily. Also, consume the crude herbal complex with *Rhus coriaria*, three capsules twice daily. Take also the juice of wild oregano, one half ounce daily.

Optional

Consume also the whole food, non-synthetic vitamin pack complex containing whole food B complex, along with vitamins A, C, and E, one packet daily. Also, increase the intake of magnesium in food. Spices, rice bran, oat bran, and nuts are top sources. Also, consuming 200 to 400 mg of chelated magnesium daily.

Chapter Ten

Diseases and Syndromes

There are a vast number of diseases and syndromes where wild oregano therapy finds great utility. For an even greater degree of information regarding its disease-fighting powers see the original wild oregano oil book in its newest edition, *The Cure is in the Cupboard* (Knowledge House Publishers, same author, available also as an audio book). A portion of these conditions are listed as follows:

Chronic fatigue syndrome

This condition is virtually always caused by deep-seated infection, the usual perpetrators being immunosuppressive viruses and the virus-like intracellular pathogen, mycoplasma. *Candida albicans* is yet another major perpetrator. Additionally, in most cases there is exhaustion of the adrenal glands as well as gross nutritional deficiency. Regardless, chronic fatigue is rapidly reversed through wild oregano therapy, especially if all three main forms are used: the oil, the aromatic juice, and the whole crude herb with *Rhus coriaria*.

Treatment protocol

Take the oil of wild oregano, five to 10 drops under the tongue or as gel caps two or three twice daily. Additionally, consume the juice of wild oregano, one half ounce twice daily, along with the whole crude herbal complex, two or more capsules twice daily.

Optional

Whole food, non-synthetic vitamin complex as packet of nine capsules, including fatty sockeye salmon oil, sunflower seed oil vitamin E, and whole food B complex caps: one packet daily, along with royal jelly combined with wild rosemary and sage, two capsules twice daily.

Candida (yeast) infection

A plague of humankind as has been demonstrated throughout this book; candida yeast is responsible for a multitude of ailments. For instance, it is a major factor behind disorders of the female genital system, including infertility, endometriosis, ovarian cysts, PMS, and, of course, vaginitis. It may also corrupt the endocrine glands, leading to a litany of symptoms. In particular yeast infestation causes stress upon the thyroid gland, leading to dysfunction of this system. A little realized fact is that candida infestation can negatively affect mood, leading to anxiety, depression, irritability, and psychosis. Additionally, the yeast is a major factor in digestive ailments, including diarrhea, chronic constipation, foul-smelling gas, bloating, indigestion, esophagitis, and irritable bowel syndrome.

Treatment protocol

Take the oil of wild oregano as drops under the tongue, five to ten drops three times daily, along with at night the whole food, natural-source probiotic complex, , tsp. in warm water at bedtime. As

well, take the whole food, crude herbal complex with *Rhus coriaria*, one or two capsules twice daily.

Optional

Consume also the whole food, non-synthetic vitamin pack complex containing whole food B complex, along with vitamins A, C, and E, one packet daily.

Migraine headaches

As demonstrated in *Natural Cures for Headaches* (Knowledge House Publishers, same author) in this condition food intolerance plays a predominant role. Foods which commonly provoke migraines include wheat, corn, cheddar cheese, Swiss cheese, cocoa, and rye. As a potent antihistamine oil of wild oregano helps halt the allergenic response, causing relief of symptoms. The oil has direct, aggressive anti-pain and anti-inflammatory properties, making it ideal for halting migraine pain. Yet another effective treatment for migraine is cannabis extract, particularly the type complexed with CO2-extracted wild oregano.

Treatment protocol

Take the oil of wild oregano as drops under the tongue, five drops repeatedly until the migraine is eliminated. It may also be rubbed topically on the temples and crown of the head. As well, take the hemp- wild oregano combination complex as sublingual drops, five or more drops as often as needed. Note: for pain syndromes the ideal type of oil of oregano to use is the ultra-potent high carvacrol formula with 84%- plus carvacrol.

Meningitis/encephalitis

Both these conditions are life-threatening, while being caused by noxious, invasive germs, a bacteria in the case of meningitis and with encephalitis, viruses. Failure to adequately diagnose, in particular, bacterial meningitis may lead to fatality or permanent damage of the brain membranes through scarring. Lyme can also result in a meningitis-like presentation. In addition to medical care in all cases the intake of high-quality, edible oil of wild oregano is invaluable and can prove lifesaving.

Treatment protocol

Take the oil of wild oregano super-strength, ideally as drops under the tongue, 20 or more drops multiple times daily. Also, rub the oil on the bottoms of the feet and up and down the shins. As well, consume the juice of wild oregano, one-ounce multiple times daily, along with whole food vitamin C complex, two capsules multiple times daily.

Multiple sclerosis

In this condition the brain is infected by various noxious agents, which cause significant damage to the nerve sheaths. This leads to, essentially, a short-circuiting of the electrical charges within the brain, explaining the various, typical symptoms. Typically, lesions known as plaque are found, these being evidence of the stripping of the fatty membrane of the myelin sheath. In some cases, the condition may be a consequence of a tick bite, where the Lyme spirochete causes destructive infection of brain and spinal cord matter.

Treatment protocol

Take the oil of wild oregano, ideally as drops under the tongue, 10 or more drops multiple times daily. Also, rub the oil on the bottoms of the feet and up and down the shins. As well, take the hemp-wild oregano

combination as sublingual drops, five or more drops as often as needed or as gel caps, two twice daily. As well, consume the juice of wild oregano, one ounce twice or more daily.

Optional

Consume the whole food, non-synthetic vitamin pack complex containing whole food B complex, along with vitamins A, C, and E, one packet daily.

Parkinson's disease

In Parkinson's disease the brain is under attack, notably by noxious pathogens known as spirochetes. For instance, as demonstrated by Lida Mattman, Ph.D., the Lyme spirochete has been found infecting the brain tissue of Parkinson's victims, as demonstrated by specialized tissue culture techniques. As many as 50% of all victims are, apparently, infected. Viruses are also causative agents, as is excessive exposure to pesticides and herbicides.

Treatment protocol

Take the oil of wild oregano, ideally as drops under the tongue, 5 to 10 drops multiple times daily. As capsules, take one or two twice daily. Also, rub the oil on the bottoms of the feet and up and down the shins as well as up and down the spine. As well, take the hemp-wild oregano combination complex as sublingual drops, ten or more drops as often as needed. Additionally, consume the juice of wild oregano, an ounce twice daily.

Optional

Consume also the whole food, non-synthetic vitamin pack complex containing whole food B complex, along with vitamins A, C, and E, one packet daily, along with two whole food, raw cannabis-wild oregano oil complex, two capsules twice daily.

Lyme disease

Lyme disease is a pandemic to the extreme, an exclusively infectious disease caused by the deer tick pathogen, *Borrelia burgdoferi*. A devastating condition, it is a major cause of a wide range of syndromes, many of which are difficult to diagnose and, thus, are not properly attributed to the cause. As demonstrated in the *Lyme Disease Cure* (same author, Knowledge House Publishers) the infection is a great mimic and is responsible for dozens of chronic, degenerative conditions, including lupus, scleroderma, fibromyalgia, Bell's palsy, multiple sclerosis, ocular disorders, rheumatoid arthritis, Alzheimer's disease, chronic fatigue syndrome, and Parkinson's disease.

Treatment protocol

Take the oil of wild oregano, 20 or more drops under the tongue multiple times daily or in juice/water, along with the whole, crude herbal complex, three capsules twice daily. As well, take the hemp-wild oregano combination complex as sublingual drops, 20 or more drops as often as needed. Consume also the juice or essence of wild oregano, an ounce or more twice daily. As well, rub the wild oregano oil, ideally a super-strength variety, up and down the spine as well as on the shins and bottoms of the feet. Note: for chronic pain, such as Lyme arthritis, the ideal type to use is the wild oregano oil ultra-formula with 84%-plus carvacrol.

Optional

Consume also the whole food, non-synthetic vitamin pack complex containing whole food B complex, along with vitamins A, C, and E, one packet daily. Take also the cannabis-turmeric complex, two or more capsules twice daily or as sublingual drops, 40 drops twice daily. As well, to build up strength for combating this condition consumed wild chaga tea with pulverized birch and tamarack bark plus wild rose hips, two or more cups daily.

Angina pectoris

Angina pectoris is a condition manifested by poor oxygenation of the blood and, particularly, the heart muscle. The lack of oxygen flow to the heart tissue causes great corruption, leading to severe or acute pain, which is known as angina. The condition may also be a sign of blockage within the arterial tree, particularly the coronary arteries. In this event the intake of natural medicines which aid blood flow and also assist in arterial wall regeneration is indicated, notably the red sour grape powder, pomegranate concentrate, and fatty whole food fish oil.

Treatment protocol

Take the oil of wild oregano as drops under the tongue, three to 10 drops as often as necessary. Also, consume the highly oxygenated juice or essence of wild oregano, a tablespoon as often as necessary.

Optional

Consume whole food fatty cod or sockeye salmon oil rich in natural-source vitamins A and D plus astaxanthin, red sour grape powder, and whole food, Mediterranean-source pomegranate concentrate.

Swollen legs (lymphatic stasis)

Swollen legs can be a consequence of a number of factors, including venous stasis, blockage of lymphatic flow, liver disease, kidney weakness/failure, and congestive heart failure. In all cases the oil is invaluable, particularly as a topical rub. Regarding heart failure both the oil and the essence aid in cardiac pumping power.

Treatment protocol

Take the oil of wild oregano, ideally, the super-strength formula as drops under the tongue or in juice/water, five to 10 drops twice daily. As well, rub the oil vigorously all over the swollen areas. Note: in many cases osteopathic manipulative therapy can be of value in reducing swelling from lymphatic and venous congestion.

Optional

Take the juice of wild oregano, one half ounce twice daily, along with the whole food, non-synthetic vitamin pack complex containing whole food B complex, along with vitamins A, C, and E, one packet daily.

Diabetes

There are a number of ways wild oregano benefits diabetics. No doubt, both the oil and the juice/essence aid in the balancing and reduction of blood sugar. The oil directly attacks many of the complications of this condition, purging fungus from the blood and also bolstering the immune system. In particular, wild oregano juice is a pancreatic tonic, which helps induce normal insulin production, while also reducing oxidation and inflammation in this organ. It has also been found to act as a hypoglycemic fully independent of insulin. Regarding the liver wild oregano extracts also help stabilize it, which is infinitely valuable for diabetes. These positive actions are enhanced by the simultaneous intake of black seed oil.

Treatment protocol

Take the oil of wild oregano, five or more drops under the tongue two or three times daily. Consume also the juice of wild oregano, one half ounce or more twice daily. Take also black seed oil, one teaspoon twice daily or, ideally, as gel caps with cumin and fennel extracts, two caps twice daily.

Optional

Consume also the whole food, non-synthetic vitamin pack complex containing whole food B complex, along with vitamins A, C, and E, one packet daily, along with the wild source chaga tea with tamarack and birch bark, two or more cups daily.

Cardiomyopathy

This condition greatly responds to oil of oregano therapy, because it is caused largely by viral infection of the heart muscle. Another factor is exposure to black mold. It is a potentially fatal condition, which is readily resolved by vigorous intake of wild oregano-based supplements, particularly the oil, whole crude herbal complex with *Rhus coriaria*, and the aromatic juice or essence. For optimal results certain supplemental nutrients should be consumed, notably vitamin D, E, and the B complex.

Treatment protocol

Take the oil of wild oregano as drops under the tongue, five to 20 drops three times daily or more often, if necessary. Also, consume the whole food, crude herbal complex with *Rhus coriaria*, three capsules twice daily, along with the aromatic juice, one ounce twice daily.

Optional

Consume also the whole food, non-synthetic vitamin pack complex containing whole food B complex, along with vitamins A, C, and E, one packet daily.

Varicose veins

A distressing condition varicose veins are related to a number of factors, including hereditary vulnerability. Of note, if they are worse on the right side or mainly present on this side, this may indicate a liver disorder, notably parasitic infestation of this organ. If they are heavy on the left, then, it may be a sign of infection of the sigmoid colon by these pathogens. The condition may also be related to nutritional deficiency, particularly a deficit of vitamins C, E, and K. Constipation is a major factor, as this leads to straining on the stool, which then causes the veins to break down and collapse.

Treatment protocol

Take the oil of wild oregano as drops under the tongue or in juice/water, five drops twice daily. Also, rub the oil vigorously over the varicosities twice or more daily.

Optional

Consume also the whole food, non-synthetic vitamin pack complex containing whole food B complex, along with vitamins A, C, and E, one packet daily.

Balding

Incredibly, balding is often caused by infestation, in this case hair follicle mites. These mites infect the roots of the hair, causing the death of the follicles. There may also be infection of the scalp by various fungi, including pityriasis, a cause of not only hair loss but also dandruff. Essentially, the fungi suffocated the hair follicles, causing their deaths. This is why the highly antifungal oil of wild oregano is so invaluable.

Treatment protocol

Take the oil of wild oregano, five drops under the tongue twice daily. Also, rub the oil topically on the scalp twice daily, supporting this by adding oregano oil to a natural, chemical free shampoo.

Hypothyroidism

A common plague, hypothyroidism is related to a number of factors, including nutritional deficiency, wrong diet, gluten intolerance, and chronic infection. Another major factor is stress, which greatly depletes the endocrine forces. As well, weakness of the pituitary and/or adrenal glands can lead to this disorder. Vitamin A deficiency is common in this condition, as is a deficit of protein and B complex.

Treatment protocol

Take the oil of wild oregano, five to 10 drops twice daily. Additionally, consume the juice of wild oregano, one tablespoon twice daily as well as a thyroid supporting herbal complex with tyrosine, kelp, and rosemary, one or two capsules twice daily.

Optional

Consume also the whole food, non-synthetic vitamin pack complex containing whole food B complex, along with vitamins A, C, and E, one packet daily.

Hyperthyroidism

In this condition the thyroid gland is hyperactive, dangerously so. Yet, what is little realized is that infestation is the main underlying cause. The infestation can be the result of viral or parasitic infection as well as mold toxicity. *Candida albicans* overload is yet another factor. As well, hyperthyroidism is associated with a number of nutritional deficiencies as well as toxicity from noxious, synthetic chemicals. Furthermore, collapse of adrenal gland function commonly results in this disorder.

Treatment protocol

Take the oil of wild oregano as drops under the tongue, five to 10 drops three times daily. Also, consume the juice or essence of wild oregano, one half ounce twice daily, along with a complex of royal jelly with rosemary and sage, two capsules twice daily. Rub the oil topically on the thyroid gland area two or three times daily. For additional therapeutic power the whole crude herb with *Rhus coriaria* can also be consumed.

Optional

Consume also the whole food, non-synthetic vitamin pack complex containing whole food B complex, along with vitamins A, C, and E, one packet daily.

Goiter

While this condition is associated with a deficiency of iodine and other key thyroid-supporting nutrients, like the B complex and vitamin A, no doubt, wild oregano is a potent natural medicine for reversing it. In fact, the essence or juice of wild oregano has been used as the front-line treatment for radiation-induced goiter.

Treatment protocol

Take under the tongue the oil of wild oregano, five or more drops twice daily, also rubbing the oil topically. As well, consume the juice or

essence of wild oregano, at least an ounce daily and in tough conditions up to three ounces daily.

Optional

Whole food vitamin A as found in wild sockeye salmon oil, three capsules twice daily.

Weak or vulnerable immune system

This is, perhaps, the most novel domain of wild oregano. Can anyone fathom its value? A weakened immune system makes the individual vulnerable to a wide range of infections, which can devastate health. Wild oregano kills every type of invasive and opportunistic pathogen. This prevents the immune system from being overloaded by such invaders. Moreover, it greatly bolsters the immune system, increasing its powers and activity against any noxious germs. For instance, it has that rare capacity to dramatically activate the white blood cells, causing them to be more efficient as germ scavengers. It also causes the induction of key enzyme elements within these cells, including glutathione peroxidase, catalase, and superoxide dismutase. Deficiencies of both vitamin C and A play a major role in immune vulnerability, as does a deficit of vitamin D and the B complex.

Treatment protocol

Take the oil of wild oregano, ideally as drops under the tongue, five or more drops twice daily. Consume also two whole food, crude herbal complex with *Rhus coriaria*, two capsules twice daily.

Optional

Consume whole food vitamin A as found in wild sockeye salmon oil, three capsules twice daily. Also take the whole food, non-synthetic vitamin pack complex containing whole food B complex, along with vitamins A, C, and E, one packet daily. Increase the consumption of top food sources of vitamin C, including citrus, spinach, broccoli, Brussels sprouts, kiwi, papaya, and tomatoes.

Hepatitis

In many cases of this disease the cause is infection, usually by viruses. It is in these types of hepatitis that wild oregano oil is most effective. In a human trial conducted by an Egyptian investigator with edible daily use oil of wild oregano was found to be more effective than standard drug therapy, significantly reversing the disease in the majority of cases.

In some 8 of 10 patients there were noticeable benefits manifested by a reduction in liver enzymes and also a significant drop in viral titers. Conducted over a two-year period, in some cases the dosage was high, up to 200 drops per day. In the majority of cases significant liver toxicity was observed at this dose. This coincides with a number of scientific studies, where the oregano oil was found to be protective for the liver, even when it is exposed to poisonous chemicals. The wild oregano therapy was found to be most effective if combined with the intake of a wild greens flushing complex, along with probiotics and black seed oil.

Treatment protocol

Take the oil of wild oregano, ideally as drops under the tongue, one or two dropperfuls three or four times daily. As well, consume the wild, raw greens flushing agent as sublingual drops, two or three dropperfuls twice daily, along with oil of black seed, Turkish source, one or two tablespoons twice daily.

Optional

Take the probiotic, teaspoon at bedtime in warm water.

Epstein-Barr infection

In this condition a virus of the herpes family attacks the body, most notably the spleen, liver, and lymphatic system. The result is typically depression and disruption of the immune system and a chronic fatigue-like syndrome. Even so, Epstein-Barr is no match for the powers of oil of wild oregano, which systematically devastates the virus, permanently purging it from the body.

Treatment protocol

Take the oil of wild oregano, ideally as drops under the tongue, 10 or more drops under the tongue multiple times daily. Also, rub the oil on the bottoms of the feet and up and down the shins. For tough conditions also consume the juice or essence of wild oregano, a half-ounce twice daily.

Autism

This condition is almost exclusively a consequence of infection. The infection arises from noxious, contaminated vaccines. Another key factor is heavy metals, particularly mercury but also aluminum, which cause damage to both the blood-brain barrier and brain tissue itself. The wild, raw greens flushing agent is also an essential element, as this helps purge such toxins from the tissues and is entirely edible, ideal for children.

Treatment protocol

Take the oil of wild oregano, a few drops twice daily. If the child will not take the oil in this manner, one gelcap per day can be given. Also, rub the oil on the bottoms of the feet and up and down the shins. As well, take the wild, raw greens flushing agent, 20 or more drops twice daily.

Optional

Consume whole food vitamin A as found in wild sockeye salmon or cod oil, three capsules twice daily.

Snake, spider, and other venomous bites

Oil of wild oregano is mandatory therapy for venomous bites, whether snake, jelly fish, scorpion, spider, or other. Simply saturate the bite site with the oil; after a half hour add more and keep saturating until all the venom is neutralized. Additionally, the oil should be taken internally.

Treatment protocol

Take the oil of wild oregano, ideally as drops under the tongue, 10 or more drops repeatedly, even every few minutes or less. As well, repeatedly saturate the site with as much oil as possible.

Dog, cat, and/or human bites

Animal bites commonly lead to infection. Such a toxicity is readily neutralized by repeated application of the wild oregano as well as internal treatment. There is no way a bite wound can become diseased or infected in presence of this potent germicidal complex.

Treatment protocol

Take the oil of wild oregano under the tongue or in juice/water, five drops two or more times daily. Also, apply the oil topically as often as necessary to prevent any infection and induce healing.

Sepsis

Sepsis or blood poisoning is a plague of modern civilization. This is particularly true as a result of the onslaught of drug-

resistant germs, whose pathogenicity is induced by the excessive use of antibiotics. Sepsis is a major killer, responsible in the United States and Canada alone for some 350,000 premature deaths, most of which occur in hospitals from antibiotic-resistant germs. Oil of wild oregano obliterates such germs and would, therefore, save countless lives if it was used aggressively routinely. Yet, it is rarely given for sepsis. When it is, it results in a dramatic cure, as demonstrated by the following case history:

CASE HISTORY:

Mr. A. was as a child and teenager completely addicted to sugar. Now, at 23, still eating refined sugar, suddenly, he developed an appendicitis attack, which commonly occurs in sugar eaters. Before the surgery could be performed the appendix burst, leading to a near fatal sepsis. His mother applied a super-strength form of oil of oregano on his feet and rubbed it repeatedly on his back and legs, while he was also given 20 drops frequently orally. Within 24 hours his fever broke, and his heart rate dropped from 124 beats per minute to normal. He was discharged without incident.

Treatment protocol

Take the oil of wild oregano as drops under the tongue 10 or more drops multiple times daily. As well, consume the essence or juice of wild oregano, one ounce twice daily. Additionally, consume the whole food, natural vitamin C complex free of all synthetic ascorbic acid, two capsules four times daily, along with whole food vitamin A in the form of wild sockeye salmon oil, three capsules three times daily.

Lupus and other autoimmune disorders

With lupus and similar autoimmune diseases there is a great derangement of the immune system. This derangement is often correlated by infection of the tissues by the yeast, *Candida albicans*, although pathogenic viruses may also play a role. One virus that may be involved is canine salivary virus, which can be contracted from dog saliva. This pathogen readily infects the skin and connective tissue, leading to the typical patterns seen in a number of autoimmune diseases, particularly lupus. In all cases of autoimmune disorders oil of wild oregano is a mainstay of treatment. No one should shy from its use to any degree. As well, for scleroderma and autoimmune thyroid disorders it is also essential to consume the aromatic juice or essence of wild oregano. This essence is also a critical therapy in autoimmune hyperthyroidism.

Treatment protocol

Take the oil of wild oregano, ideally, five or more drops under the tongue twice daily. As well, consume the juice or essence of wild oregano, a half ounce once or twice daily.

Optional

Consume whole food vitamin A as found in wild sockeye salmon oil, three capsules twice daily, along with a whole food B complex powder with torula yeast and rice bran, two tablespoons daily.

How long do I take it?

This is one of the most common questions asked regarding wild oregano oil therapy. This varies. Yet, as a rule the individual should continue the recommended dose until there is noticeable improvement, then reducing that dose by 50% or more. A reasonable time span is 60 to 80 days or longer. If necessary, maintenance dosing may be as little as one-third or less of the initial recommendation. For chronic conditions a daily long-term dose of the truly edible, wild type is reasonable, one capsule or 5 to 10 drops daily.

Chapter Eleven

Bonus Uses

Isn't *101 Uses* sufficient? Incredibly, oil of wild oregano and other wild oregano-based supplements offer even a greater plethora of benefits. Regardless, who would ever think that a single, all-natural, wild substance could offer such a diversity of uses? The fact is the breadth of its benefits and the immense utility of its applications, makes oil of wild oregano the first choice in natural medicines, the most potent, broad-spectrum of all: the most versatile natural remedy known.

Air cleansing and aromatherapy

In the air there are a number of challenges which confront people. There are pathogens, which can, upon inhalation, readily cause symptoms and diseases. There are also various allergens, also disease- and symptom-causing. Too, there are odors which can be noxious and bothersome, even irritating to the point of causing reactions and symptoms. Here, wild oregano oil is a boon. So are certain other spice oil-like complexes, including oils of wild lavender and bay leaf. Regarding the oil it can be added to a diffuser. It can also be burned, as on a candle or even rubbed on a lightbulb. The latter is an invaluable way to decontaminate the air in a motel. The oil can also be put on a heat-resistant dish and gently heated in a low oven or over a stove. The point is people can fumigate their way to better health through the wild oregano oil.

Travel aid: food- and water-borne disease prevention and more

Here is where wild oregano oil is exceedingly invaluable and even lifesaving. When traveling, a wide range of disasters can occur, particularly the contraction of infectious disease from tainted food and water. This can not only ruin the trip but also greatly corrupt the health, in many cases permanently. There is also a risk for fatality from such foreign-borne food and water infections. There is no reason to endure this. All that is necessary is to regularly consume, fastidiously so, the oil of wild oregano with each meal and to also, of course, be cautious of the food and beverages consumed. To supplement this, it is necessary to take a probiotic, ideally the highly potent, vigorously implanting 500 strain.

Treatment protocol

With each meal take the oil of wild oregano, five to 10 drops, along with, ideally, the multiple spice oil capsules, one or two with each meal. As well, consume the vigorously implanting probiotic complex, teaspoon twice daily. Be sure also to take the oil twice daily, as well as the probiotic, for at least a week prior to any potentially suspect journey. Another powerful therapy is the multiple spice oil complex, highly protective, one or two capsules with each meal.

Lymphatic mobilization and massage

There is no superior mobilization agent of the lymph fluids than oil of wild oregano. Aggressively, it causes lymph fluid movement, unblocking all congestion. Sites of lymphatic congestion include the lower legs, tops of the feet, over the sacrum, pit of the low back, above the clavicles, and about the breasts as well as under the armpits. Moreover, a person doesn't have to have an obvious swelling to suffer from stagnation of this fluid. All people suffer from a degree of lymphatic toxicity and congestion. This is why a routine rubbing of the body with oil of wild oregano is health- sustaining.

Methodology

Vigorously rub the oil of wild oregano over any site of lymphatic congestion. Alternatively, rub the oil on the bottoms of the feet, top of the feet, up and down the shins, and up and down the spine. Other sites of rubbing include about the sacrum and about the breasts. The lymphatic fluids dump in an area just underneath the clavicles, so the area just above and below these bones is also an optimal site for oregano oil rubbing. The ideal types to use topically are the super-strength formulation and/or the ultra-oregano oil blend with 84%-plus carvacrol.

Tenderizing meat and flavoring foods

What a fascinating benefit of wild oil of oregano, which is its culinary use. Here, it can act to flavor foods in tiny amounts, like a drop or two or three in a marinara or pizza sauce or as a component of marinades. Yet, a little-known power relates to potentially tough meat, especially poultry. By rubbing the carcass with the oil, the meat will be fully tenderized. This is especially true of baked poultry. It can also be used as a rub for ribs and potentially tough steaks. The oil may also be added to cheese dips for a sharp flavor. Add the contents of the whole, crude herb capsules to marinades and also cheese dips and soups. Be creative with wild oregano: for your better health.

Water cleansing and activation

There may occur times when the only water available for consumption is not potable. Here, wild oregano oil can prove invaluable. Typically, in an emulsified form in extra virgin olive oil it takes about a 3% solution to thoroughly sterilize water. At the same time the oregano oil actives the oxygen molecules in the water. In this regard it can be added to normal, healthy spring water or filtered tap water but at a lower dose, like a half percent or less.

Methodology

In potentially disease-bearing water add the oil of wild oregano, ideally a super-strength form, five or more drops for every ounce of water. Thus, for an eight-ounce glass of water a person must add about 40 drops or one dropperful. For a gallon of water, it is necessary to add about a half bottle of a one-ounce bottle of oregano oil. After adding to the container shake vigorously and thoroughly.

Vulnerability to peanut allergy

What could be worse than to eat a natural food and in consequence endure such a serious reaction as to become hospitalized and nearly die? Or, what about actually suffering a fatality from eating it? This is true of those who are reactive to peanuts and/or its nut butter. Yet, no longer do such reactive people need to be concerned, including sensitized children. Oil of wild oregano, edible type, daily use will fully resolve this. Note: be sure that for this purpose only the original, whole food, wild-source oregano oil is used, as this is a guaranteed therapy for preventing the serious consequences of anaphylactic shock and could never aggravate the condition. In contrast, with imitation brands, especially those derived from farm-raised oregano and/or false oregano species, there is a risk for additional reactivity.

Treatment protocol

Take the oil of wild oregano, ideally as drops under the tongue, for prevention, three to five drops twice daily or as gel caps, one or two daily. To combat an acute peanut allergy reaction, take the oil every few minutes or less, a few drops at a time. As well, for prevention consume the whole crude herb complex, one or two capsules daily.

GMO intoxication neutralization

Make no mistake GMOs are systematically polluting the people: in a major way to a massive degree. When the GMOs are consumed, they must be neutralized. Otherwise, they may readily cause symptoms and disease. The primary GMOs to avoid are commercial soy, cottonseed, canola, corn, beet sugar, and their derivatives, although animal foods, like eggs and meat, from cattle or poultry fed GMOs is also tainted.

Treatment protocol

To neutralize and detoxify GMOs take the edible, daily use oil of wild oregano, five drops with each meal, and in the event of major exposure, five to 10 drops three or more times daily. As well, consume the digestive-aiding whole food, crude herbal complex with *Rhus coriaria*, two capsules two or more times daily.

Vaccine toxicity syndrome

The toxicity of vaccines is extreme, in fact, beyond comprehension. They are not only noxious but also potentially fatal. Each year in North America alone thousands of individuals die directly from inoculations, many from sudden death syndromes. These sudden deaths occur mainly in infants and toddlers. However, this can also occur in older children, like four- to ten-year-olds.

Vaccines also cause a more methodical, treacherous type of death: that from chronic, degenerative disease. The fact is these injections are directly related to the onset of diabetes, particularly type 1, autoimmune disorders, rheumatoid arthritis, multiple sclerosis, paralysis, asthma, eczema, lupus, and cancer, particularly lymphoma, brain cancer, bone cancer, and leukemia. This is largely because the inoculations cause smoldering infections which suppress the immune system, allowing these diseases to develop. For those who have been burdened by heavy doses all efforts must be made to purge vaccine toxins from the body, particularly any infectious agents which were introduced through the injections.

Make no mistake people who are injected with inoculations are grossly contaminated. This includes heavy contamination with carcinogens, including highly invasive tumor-inducing viruses. All such viruses must be purged from the body in order to prevent vaccine-induced carcinoma.

As well, there must be an effort made to detoxify vaccinations in case they are imposed upon people against their will. Oil of wild oregano is crucial in this regard, as it must be applied topically to the injection site and also taken both before and after the inoculation as sublingual

drops. Additionally, the intake of certain nutrients is critical, particularly vitamins A and C, which protect against vaccine toxicity.

Treatment protocol

To protect the body from inevitable inoculation, take the oil of wild oregano as drops under the tongue, five to ten drops two or more times daily. As well, apply the oil directly on any injection site. Additionally, take the whole food vitamin C complex, two capsules twice daily or for children in powdered form, teaspoon daily. To purge existing vaccine overload, take the oil of wild oregano, five or more drops three times daily, along with the essence or juice of wild oregano, one or more tablespoon twice daily. Follow this protocol for at least 90 days as a full- body purge.

Optional

Take the total body purging agent as a liquid complex in a 12-ounce bottle, one ounce daily for at least thirty days and for children, a half-ounce daily. As well, consume whole food vitamin A as found in wild sockeye salmon oil, three capsules twice daily or for children, one or two teaspoons daily.

Cancer prevention and treatment

Make no mistake oil of oregano and its hydrosol essence are highly anti-carcinogenic. Within the oregano oil it is the terpenes and long-chain alcohols which offer potent antitumor properties as well as the simple phenol carvacrol itself. Carvacrol, too, is a potent antitumor agent. Studies have shown that this substance has a direct effect to block tumor cell growth. Another marker, found in leukemia, that is thrombin, was also blocked by oregano, in this case components of the whole, crude herb.

It is even more profound than this. In a study published by Italian investigators an extract of wild oregano was found to be directly toxic to cancer cells, in this case those which cause colon cancer. There was an arrest of tumor growth. The cell death was attributed to an increase in the production of the highly protective enzyme, glutathione peroxidase. The spice extract, the researchers found, triggered various mechanisms leading to obliteration of the cancerous cells, known as apoptosis. Curiously, the researchers found that only the whole, unprocessed complex, that is the full spectrum of components found in either the whole, crude herb or the steam-distilled oil, was effective in tumor destruction, not any single component. In other words, a single component, like carvacrol, never equals the whole. Note: this is not a recommendation by any company of a cure but, rather, merely information based upon freedom of speech: an interpretation of the available science for the sake of humans in need.

Treatment protocol

For cancer prevention use both the oil of oregano and its aromatic waters, the juice of wild oregano, about five drops of the oil once or twice daily or as gel caps, one twice daily, along with a half-ounce of the juice daily. For treatment and/or for aiding in orthodox therapy the dose must be higher, like 20 or more drops three times daily, while also consuming the juice, one or more ounces twice daily, and the whole, crude herb with *Rhus coriaria,* three or more capsules twice daily. Note: for topical use the ultra-formula with 84%-plus carvacrol is ideal.

Cold/flu prevention

It was through the book *The Cure is in the Cupboard* that the powers of oil of oregano for cold/flu prevention was

discovered. Regardless, why get a cold or a case of the flu if it can be completely prevented? To achieve this all a person needs to do is take the wild oregano oil on a daily basis. Even if taken every other day it is effective. Yet, during potentially high risk cold and/or flu season daily intake or even twice daily consumption is advised. The study published in *Antiviral Research* demonstrates the mechanism, which is that a modest amount of oil of oregano or other highly antiseptic spice oils, like oils of sage and cumin, block the growth of infectious viruses in the bloodstream. In other words, if the spice oil components are continuously in the blood or, possibly, within the mucous membranes there is no way the pathogenic viruses can multiply. This was the first time in history that any such data was published, which amounts to a proof for the use of these natural spice oil complexes in prevention of colds and flu.

Another preventive substance is the whole food vitamin C made from wild camu camu plus rose hips and acerola. This entirely natural complex should be taken on a daily basis along with the oregano oil. Another preventive option is the intake of natural-source vitamin C from citrus. The fact is the daily consumption of fresh, whole oranges, grapefruits, lemons, and/or limes is a highly effective preventive.

As well, vitamins A and D are required for optimal immunity. Their regular intake provides a significant defense against viral invasion. In this regard sunlight, which induces vitamin D synthesis, is also a defense. The regular intake of vitamins A and D is necessary for protecting the body against the ravages of these diseases.

As well, for those particularly vulnerable to cold/flu there is another wild oregano-based supplement that is of value. This is the multiple spice oil complex dry capsule, which can be taken daily such as one capsule every morning or one capsule twice daily.

Treatment protocol

Take oil of wild oregano, three to five drops daily. Also, consume the multiple spice oil complex capsules, one or two capsules daily. As well, take a whole food vitamin C complex with camu camu, acerola, and rosehips, free of all synthetic sources, one or two capsules daily.

Optional

Consume also the whole food, non-synthetic vitamin pack complex containing whole food B complex, along with vitamins A, C, and E, one packet daily. As well, consume the whole food vitamin A and D source, wild sockeye salmon oil, two or more capsules twice daily.

Elimination of sugar cravings

Sugar cravings are largely caused as a result of infestation of the body by yeasts and fungi. The intake of this noxious, false food leads to the overgrowth of these organisms, and the organisms, then, create a toxicity which leads to what is often uncontrollable cravings. Another cause is an imbalance in the glands, notably the adrenals, though this, too, is the result of sugar consumption. There is an attempt after eating this poison to artificially raise blood sugar levels, which explains the relentless cravings. Plus, oregano oil and the aromatic juice have been shown to regulate blood sugar levels, acting as if artificial insulin.

Treatment protocol

Take the oil of wild oregano, ideally as drops under the tongue, five or more drops multiple times. Also, increase the consumption of cinnamon with meals. Another aid is the multiple spice oil mix with oils of fenugreek, myrtle, cumin, cinnamon, sage and oregano, 5 or more drops as needed.

Radiation poisoning and toxicity

For radiation toxicity wild oregano has a number of uses. This includes the damage and destruction induced by radiotherapy as is administered in cancer victims. For radiation burns oregano oil minimizes scarring, while also speeding healing. Additionally, it prevents infection from occurring in radiation-induced wounds. Taken internally, its potent antioxidants block the typical oxidation damage which occurs as a result of radiological ions. In the event of damage to the thyroid, whether by medical X-rays or radiation accidents, the spice is invaluable, with the juice of wild oregano being a most potent therapy for reversing thyroid damage.

Treatment protocol

In the event of exposure to radiation and/or radiological injury consume the oil of wild oregano, five or more drops twice daily, along with the juice of wild oregano, one or more ounces daily. Additionally, take the whole crude herb complex with *Rhus coriaria*, two or more capsules twice daily. For actual radiation burns apply the oil topically repeatedly. As well, increase the consumption of vitamin C and protein, including sources of collagen.

Elimination of tobacco cravings

Destructive beyond belief, every effort possible must be taken to obliterate the habit of regular tobacco smoking. This includes the intake of its toxins through chewing and also second-hand smoke. Oil of wild oregano is a powerful therapy in this regard. By taking it as sublingual drops it reduces and in many cases eliminates the desire for smoking or chewing. Another sublingual formula that is effective is the cannabis-wild oregano complex. Taken sublingually, it is a most potent means to eliminate craving, while enhancing a sensation of wellness, including mental stability. No doubt, the wild oregano-hemp plant extract combination is one of the most potent natural therapeutic complexes known for eliminating nicotine-based addictions.

Treatment protocol

Take the oil of wild oregano as drops under the tongue, three drops three times daily, taking it also whenever enduring tobacco cravings. As well, take the CO2-extract wild hemp-wild oregano complex, three to five drops under the tongue as often as needed or as gel caps, one three times daily.

Reduction in food cravings and prevention of over-eating

No doubt, the majority of people overeat, essentially, eating themselves into the grave. One reason for this is the overgrowth of fungi and yeasts in the body, which cause cravings for food, notably sugar and starch. Parasites also induce cravings, which may be manifested by constant or insatiable hunger. Oddly, in some cases parasitic infestation can lead to the opposite, which is a suppression of appetite.

Treatment protocol

Take three to five drops of oil of wild oregano before each meal. As well, take two capsules of the whole food, crude herbal complex with each meal.

Optional

Consume also the whole food, non-synthetic vitamin pack complex containing whole food B complex, along with vitamins A, C, and E, one packet daily.

Reduction in cravings for drugs

What a debacle it is to be addicted to either illicit or prescription drugs. In all such cases the intake of the oil as sublingual drops will curb the cravings. This is, in part, because of its rich content of the neuron-activating terpene, beta caryophyllene. This is the same terpene in cannabis which accounts for its anti-addictive nature, that is its capacity to reduce the desire for hard drugs. Then, too, the hemp-cannabis CO2 extract complexed with wild oregano is an ideal adjunct for eliminating drug cravings, including craving for extremely powerful street drugs, like cocaine, crack, and heroin.

Treatment protocol

Take the oil of oregano under the tongue, five drops three times daily, also taking it at any urge or desire for drug intake. As well, consume a hemp oil-wild oregano combination, five to 10 drops three times daily, taking it, as well, for any cravings.

Chapter Twelve

Wild Oregano Testimonials

There are a number of revealing reports arising from users which demonstrate the immense powers of wild oregano therapy. These testimonials are, essentially, mini-clinical trials. They can be regarded with much import, as they usually involve sufferers of chronic conditions who have attempted a number of modalities and have found little hope, getting minimal to no results until taking the oregano therapy. The testimonials are mainly in regard to the use of the emulsified oil in an extra virgin olive oil base, although some of these describe benefits from the whole, crude herbal complex as well as the aromatic essence.

It will be evident that in these testimonials the brand names are redacted. This is in keeping with certain mandates at the federal level. The purpose is to allow the information to be disseminated freely, while protecting companies from potential action taken. At this time direct endorsements by brands regarding medical conditions is limited to so-called structure-function claims, with disease-associated statements being restricted.

Severe case of intractable bronchitis reversed with oil of wild oregano therapy Ms. K. is a 60-year-old woman who is allergic to cigarette smoke. After exposure to heavy smoking in Europe she traveled on a flight where smoking was allowed. Shortly thereafter, she developed a severe case of bronchitis with intractable coughing. Nothing eased the symptoms until she took a massive amount of wild oregano oil gel caps, 25 all at once. Suddenly, the symptoms abated, including the horrific cough, and the condition was fully resolved.

Woman using the original, truly Mediterranean- source brand for 15 years never gets sick until she switches brands Ms. D. described how for 15 years she has stayed free of all cold and flu symptoms from the regular intake of truly whole food, wild oregano oil. With her vulnerable immune system, she found the oil highly protective. When she ran out, her son convinced her to try another brand. Upon doing so, for the first time in over a decade, suddenly, she developed cold-flu symptoms; in other words, she actually had a negative result from the intake of the off-brand, and as a result swore she would never again consume such inferior supplements.

10-year case of tinnitus reversed with small amount of oil of wild oregano Mr. G. has suffered with tinnitus for over a decade. Reasoning that it was caused by sinus congestion and/or fungal infection he took a course of wild oregano oil therapy. After simply taking three drops twice daily within a week all symptoms of his tinnitus had disappeared.

Childhood eczema reversed with whole crude herbal complex with Rhus coriaria Ms. D. reported that she had two children with mild-to-moderate eczema. As well, the children suffered from weakened immune system. Given the contents of three capsules daily within two months in both instances the eczema was cleared.

Multiple boils all over body and scalp eliminated through heavy dosing of a super-strength grade of wild oregano oil Mr. H., a respected golf pro, suffered boils all over his body. The boil condition largely resulted from the overuse of antibiotics, along with multiple hospitalizations. It was a case where this caused him nearly complete hair loss. After hearing about the original book on wild oregano on the radio, *The Cure is in the Cupboard*, he purchased the book and began taking the oregano, the whole, crude herb with *Rhus coriaria*, along with a super-strength grade of oil. Using large doses, also rubbing the oil on his scalp and body, within 90 days all the boils had disappeared. As a bonus the hair on his scalp began growing back.

Massive warts disappear on wild oregano therapy

F. O. reported regarding her daughter: "Having used oregano oil on my daughter's huge wart on her knee—she'd had them for about three years, and I couldn't get rid of them no matter what I'd tried, until I tried the wild, original Mediterranean source brand (brand-name redacted to generic). Within three weeks they (that is the warts) had disappeared, never to return. Our family will never go without this oil. What happened to my daughter was a miracle."

COPD case gets relief immediately

Rachel W. reported: "Thank you for (brand name redacted). It has been a lifesaver. Having been diagnosed with COPD years ago, I was dependent on oxygen for breath. Not anymore. Having heard on TV that wild oregano is good for the lungs, I immediately bought some. Luckily, it was (brand name redacted). It was the best thing that ever happened to me. It started improving my breathing immediately. I am now off all oxygen and can function normally, doing things I haven't done in years.

She added, "I thank God and people like you, who researched the resources and put on this Earth this lifesaving product: for healing all nations. Keep up the work, and God bless you all."

Ms. Louise Z. 's impacted wisdom tooth is cured

Ms. Z.'s testimonial is verbatim, as follows:

I am writing this letter to give you a testimonial for your oil of oregano, (brand name redacted), and to thank you, again, for your wonderful books. I had a fully impacted wisdom tooth under my gums for many years, which had never given me any problems until recently, when my dentist discovered inflammation in my gums. He said it was this tooth and that I must go to an oral surgeon to remove it. He stated that I would probably lose two other molars in the process. I found out about the oil of oregano and (company name redacted) at a health food store, where a girl recommended the book, *The Cure is in the Cupboard.*

I began using the oil, brushing my teeth with it and massaging it into my gums. The wisdom tooth broke through the skin and started to grow and grow. The dentist said the tooth was still impacted, but I would not give up putting the oil on the gums and teeth. It started to get loose.

Eleven months later the wisdom tooth and root rolled out of my mouth: no bleeding, no pain.

My doctor said it was a miracle. The dentist couldn't believe what happened, he said that in his 50 years of practice, he had never seen a fully impacted wisdom tooth fall out on its own.

It was your oil of wild oregano that gave such a happy ending to this story. Thank you again.

Man, who suffered for years from antibiotic overuse gets major relief

Mr. Martin P. said: "As a victim of antibiotic therapy for various illnesses through the years and subsequent chronic yeast infections, the wonders of your products never cease to amaze me. Specifically, at this time I have been using the oil to treat a rosacea condition in my eyes that caused dry eye syndrome. As a result of the condition, I was placed on yet another antibiotic, which caused a rebound of the yeast infection as well as vertigo. The yeast was controlled by oil of wild oregano and the whole,

crude herbal formula with *Rhus coriaria* (brand name redacted). Now, I am taking two drops of the oil, morning and night, and one capsule three times daily. As a result, my yeast infection is under control."

Woman has overnight success with wild oregano, calling it "incredible"R. Harth said: "I had a bladder infection, which bothered me terribly. Recently, I began using (brand name redacted) capsules twice daily, and I am happy to report my bladder infection has completely cleared up. I have also used oil of oregano to treat a skin rash. It cleared up the rash overnight. This wild oregano is incredible."

Mr Hurwitz says wild oregano is better than 'advertised'Mr. Hurwitz' testimonial is verbatim, as follows:

"I'm 60 years-old and am very pleased with the wild oregano supplements. I use (brand name redacted) oil of wild oregano, and it has cleared up my nail fungus. My energy levels have also improved. Finally, I have found a product that does everything that it says it will do—and more."

Man with over six conditions gets relief for all with wild oregano treatmentM. Rosky suffered a combination of rosacea, candida overload, circulatory disorders, allergic intolerance, chronic fatigue syndrome, and migraines. According to Mr. Rosky:

"After trying (brand name redacted) oil of oregano, I have never again used antibiotics or aspirin or any other over-the-counter drug or prescription medication. They have given me my life back. I know from the bottom of my heart how much these products have helped me."

He continued, "I will never stop using it or this particular brand, because I know how safe it is to use, even on your skin. I did try another brand one time, and although it was less expensive, it was also very dangerous.

I took it internally which caused severe stomach pain and also tried some on my skin, which I could hardly stop it from burning. You never have any of these problems with the products from (company name redacted). Quality is very important to me, and what I put into my body is even more important. I guess you get what you pay for. Many products try to imitate the true oil of oregano oil are nothing other than cheap imitations. Thanks a million for your wonderful products."

Ron Turpin reported the following about three different people helped by the juice of wild oregano: He first took it himself. "When I began taking it, taking the first dose, my head cleared up in 10 minutes or less. I slept better at night, although my wife still hacked and coughed as usual." Turpin reported that the juice had fully cleared up his sinus and allergy symptoms. He then said, "After noticing my success my skeptical wife, in desperation, tried it. Guess what, she is now a confirmed wild oregano user. The juice of oregano cleared up her sinus problems. She no longer coughed all the time. She began noticing other improvements. No longer did she take the daily dose of allergy pills. Her headaches disappeared. She mentioned one day that she no longer needed indigestion pills. One day I was putting on my shoes and I called my wife: 'Come look at my feet.' All the ugly calluses and dry, ugly skin was gone. My feet were pink and smooth. My nails, which were previously thick and brown, had lightened up, returning to normal."

"I told my friends about it, and they are now confirmed juice of wild oregano users. My wife's best friend tried it, and she said it was the first time in six years she was able to sleep all night. Also, she had a bladder and urinary tract problem, which caused her to get up several times each night. After a few days on the juice, all this returned to normal.

I can't recall any prescription drug as effective as the oil of wild oregano. It acts unbelievably fast, without side effects. I talked to yet another one of my friends this morning, and he said he considered it a miracle. Thanks a million for this great product."

Man in public eye gets relief through wild spice face-lift

Taking a tip from his esthetician Mr. M. decided that it was worth a try to use oil of wild oregano, topically, for a new cystic acne breakout. Within a week the acne was eradicated, which was predicted by the esthetician, who well knew its powers. "I had my doubts," he noted, "but I tried it and it worked."

Mr. M. added, "As a professional who cannot hide my face from many, many people every single day, this was humiliating and made me not want to come to work. Moreover, when I was at work, it made me want to hide in my office. Though I gave this a shot on a whim, it worked and did so quickly. In fact, the acne was gone within days. This was life- changing: cystic acne, gone. (The lesions) flattened, the color fading after just one to two days: gone within a week."

As an important note for those who are reluctant to use, for instance, the super-strength grade or any oil of oregano topically, especially on the face, he said:

"I have super-sensitive skin and using it directly at full strength didn't even bother it, though I made sure not to put it on any broken skin."

Man with chronic sinus infection sees full results in a single days Mr. D. suffered for years with chronic sinus infections, using drug therapy with no results. He reported a most astounding consequence:

"Using super-strength oil of oregano, I knocked out a chronic sinus infection in 24 hours. I took one or two eyedroppers two or more times daily. After that I noticed that I relieved a recurrent yeast infection—without any antifungal creams.

The yeast infection and the sinus trouble were persistent and reoccurring, because of an autoimmune syndrome, known as Sjogren's syndrome or dry eye sicca. I have had chronic dry eye, a very harsh and severe case of it, for years. After the first one-ounce bottle of super-strength I noticed a slight improvement with my dry eye syndrome. After I used another bottle of the super-strength I had an amazing improvement in my dry eye syndrome. I could now go out in the sun whenever I wanted. I do credit this fine supplement for obliterating my bleeding sinus infection in less than six hours: all by itself, while also eliminating my skin yeast infections yet also, incredibly, the dry eye syndrome."

Whole, crude herb formula with Rhus coriaria clears up chronic bladder condition and skin disorder

Ms. J. suffered for years with a chronic bladder disorder, usually bacterial in origin, along with an eczema-like skin rash. Taking only the whole, wild oregano herb complex with *Rhus coriaria* she gained a full reversal of these conditions, stating that she was "happy to report that (her) bladder infection completely cleared up," and the "skin rash cleared up overnight," adding that wild oregano is "incredible."

Man with severe toxicity from overseas traveling gets full recovery with edible, daily use wild oregano oil Mr. B. contracted while traveling to the Mediterranean severe infections of the digestive system, along with hepatitis C. Symptoms included agonizing stomach pain, nose bleeds, internal bleeding, rashes, diarrhea, and vomiting. No doctor could determine the entire cause or treatment, even suggesting that he see a psychiatrist. Mr. B. had lost 40 pounds and was in a desperate condition.

His son purchased the edible, daily use, original brand of oil of wild oregano. after taking it for two weeks, "every symptom vanished." He also noticed more restful sleep, smoother skin, and improved digestion.

Woman with low energy gets power and strength from juice of wild oregano and oil combination Ms. P., who is a big fan of the oil of wild oregano, began combining it with the wild oregano juice. As soon as she started taking it she noticed an immediate difference. She was able to do outdoor activities with energy to last. Since taking the two together, she reported, she was able to run errands that lasted four hours, which never happened before without her becoming completely exhausted and, thus, cutting the day short." He was so enthused at the results that she ordered 12 bottles of juice, along with a few bottles of super-strength oil. This combo, she says, gave her a new life with a vitality she never before experienced.

Chronic colitis eliminated with combination of oil and whole, crude herbal complex Mr. C. suffered from irritable bowel for decades. Hearing about the fungal connection to the disease he decided to take the wild oregano oil and the whole, crude herbal complex with *Rhus coriaria* daily, the oil in a dose of five to ten drops three times daily, the capsules at three twice daily. Incredibly, within one week the colitis symptoms were obliterated, an impressive result for a chronic condition of over 20 years.

Woman with dangerous return of basal cell skin cancer sees eradication with super-strength type oil of wild oregano Mr. N. is a cancer sufferer who has gone through much stress with a variety of health conditions. There was now further stress when a basal cell cancer removal proved inadequate, and the cancer began re- developing. In desperation she applied regularly a super-strength form of oil of wild oregano to the lesion. To her happy astonishment the basal cell cancer was eradicated in a mere 10 days.

Man with abdominal distress and cramping, possibly food-related poisoning, gets benefits from applying oil of wild oregano topically Mr. I., who is an avid fan of wild oregano therapy, got to test its powers for a unique concern; he had consumed old food in the refrigerator that was apparently contaminated with mold. Within eight hours he is developing rumbling and gurgling in his abdomen and also tight gas. Taking the oregano oil under the tongue he didn't get full relief. He resorted to rubbing large amounts all over his abdomen. Helping him fall asleep by the time he awoke all his symptoms had disappeared.

Chapter Thirteen

Conclusion

Oil of wild oregano is a godsend, a great gift for the benefit of humankind. The merciful, sophisticated creator produced this natural medicine as a universal antiseptic. This means that for all manner of infections the individual can rely only one basic source, high-grade wild oregano oil, the daily use type, for the cure.

This surely simplifies all issues. Regardless of the infectious source, whether viral, bacterial, fungal, or parasitic, wild oregano is the answer. It is, no doubt, the most potent antiviral agent known. Moreover, it is the only natural medicine capable of destroying all types of molds and fungi, even the notoriously noxious black mold as well as *Candida albicans.* It is also a most potent antibacterial agent available, surely equal to any antibiotic and in most cases far superior: without even the least possibility of side effects. Regarding the latter, once again, this is true of the daily use formula exclusively, where the oregano oil is derived exclusively from the wild-growing, true oregano species.

Even so, what other natural medicine can achieve this degree of efficacy? Which one could even remotely do so?

As well, is there even a single drug which has this level of power and diversity? Here, some 120-plus uses have been described. Yet, there are countless dozens of other applications, which aren't even listed. Perhaps the reader knows of numerous other benefits and uses wild oregano offers. The discussion of these is welcome on any forum, blog, or Website, where natural medicines are delineated. Or, ideally, an individual may write or email this publisher and describe these uses. This is so they may be added to a future edition of this book. An email address directly to the author is as follows: contact@purelywildnatu ral.com.

Let us review this plethora of benefits which wild oregano offers. In any respiratory ailment wild oregano is the therapy of choice, particularly the oil and the water- phase essence. These powerful extracts decimate colds and flu, while even reversing pneumonia, even the life-threatening type. Regarding bronchitis, oil of wild oregano is highly potent, purging all traces of it, while preventing any recurrences. For sinusitis, whether consumed internally or applied directly into the sinus cavities, it is the only efficient natural medicine for achieving a rapid result. Even chronic lung diseases, such as pulmonary fibrosis, COPD, asthma, tuberculosis, and emphysema, respond to its immense medicinal powers.

For digestive disorders wild oregano is a major therapeutic intervention, which has been used in this regard for thousands of years. Some 5000 years ago it was known to reverse stomach-ache and dyspepsia, while halting diarrhea. Now, it is known that it is a front-line therapy for GERD and H. pylori as well as gastritis and esophagitis. People would not think that it is healthy for the delicate esophagus; even so, wild oregano is precisely the remedy they need. Yet, too,

as has been recently confirmed wild oregano is a lead therapy for disorders of the intestines, the list, here, also being thorough: irritable bowel syndrome, ulcerative colitis, Crohn's disease, diverticulitis, leaky gut syndrome, chronic diarrhea, anal fistula, and far more.

Regarding the liver, kidneys, and pancreas oregano oil is exceptional, aiding function in every way, while never causing any harm. In some cases, the intake of the oil, combined with the whole crude herbal complex and in some cases the juice, completely reverses diseases in these organs. For these delicate organs this is true exclusively of the edible type derived from the wild, high-mountain species that grows on the rocky slopes along the Fertile Crescent region. The types that are grown in soil or which are derived from non-oregano species rich in thymol do not have this universal safety. In this regard it must be kept in mind that both thymus and marjoram species are often sold as oregano oil, since the latter is in demand and is highly marketable. These imitation oregano oils are unfit for human consumption, particularly for daily use. Do not be confused by unscrupulous marketeers, who sell inferior supplements and who, in fact, are not even scrutinizing the quality of the raw materials. This includes so-called private label brands, where there is no quality control of any kind and where the source is unidentifiable. It surely also includes all so-called standardized types. There is no way, naturally, to standardize carvacrol levels. Also, beware of those types, including certain oregano oil gel caps, tainted with GMOs, including soy lecithin.

Regarding the latter the claim is that such lecithin is non- GMO. This is marketing hype, a mere attempt to bamboozle the public. The fact is the lecithin that is being used is from GM soy. It is heavily processed, so that there is a false claim that is made: that the GMOs are 'processed out,' which is false. This is so companies may use GMOs, while attempting to deceive the gullible, vulnerable public.

For skin health wild oregano oil is also most potent, with the oil alone obliterating countless dermatological conditions, many of which are mentioned here. It is a universal remedy for supposedly incurable conditions, like seborrhea, rosacea, and acne. It also keeps the skin health helping block, even reverse, the aging process.

The immune system, too, is a major beneficiary, with oregano oil therapy cleansing this system, allowing it to function at its maximum capacity. It also boosts the capacity of the immune cells to scavenge and purge noxious germ which largely explains its powers as a daily preventive. Once again, the edible, daily use oil complex is fully ideal for human consumption, which cannot be said of imitation brands where there is a lack of such rigorous quality control.

It's a similar issue for cancer prevention, where the data has shown that daily or routine use is highly protective. This is particularly true of colon, pancreatic, and liver cancer as well as cancers of the immune organs, like leukemia and lymphoma. As well, daily use, as well as application topically, is preventive against skin carcinogenesis.

The heart also benefits from oregano oil therapy, as do the arteries. All infectious conditions of the heart and arteries respond, including cardiomyopathy, bacterial endocarditis, pericarditis, and arteritis as well as Raynaud's syndrome. There should be no hesitation to take the oregano oil in heart disease, even for those on medication. It is, after all, a GRAS substance, which means generally regarded as safe for all people. In hypertension there is a minor issue,

where on occasion the oil may cause a temporary rise in blood pressure. This is because oil of wild oregano increases the pumping power of the heart. This rise may be combated in a simple way, that is by taking the oil with a full meal. Another technique to use is to put it in a shot glass of extra virgin olive oil. Turning it into slow release, usually this modest reaction is eliminated. As well, putting the oil in black seed oil also halts this reaction, as the former is highly anti-hypertensive.

Another issue relates to the good bacteria. High dose oregano therapy may kill a portion of these health-giving organisms. In such a case it is essential to increase the intake of fermented foods and also to take higher amounts of probiotics in order to maintain gut flora balance. This is not an issue with low dose therapy, like a few drops once or twice daily.

While it is not commonly realized in the realm of cancer treatment, as well as prevention, wild oregano is a powerhouse. This is true of all its forms but especially the oil, the supercritical extract, and the aromatic essence. Yet, the wild spice itself is preventive, as is its associated wild herb, *Rhus coriaria*. The data is clear. Wild oregano is highly anti-carcinogenic. According to Greek investigators working at the University of Thessaloniki it directly destroys tumor cells, including cancer cell lines. The work was confirmed by Fan and his group in *Anticancer Drugs*, where the oregano oil active component carvacrol was found to be so potent that it was recommended to be used as an anticancer drug. Other researchers have found that it indirectly induces cancer cell death through its power of enhancing the synthesis of anti-cancer enzymes, for instance, glutathione and SOD. Plus, it offers the value of topical application, where it can be used both for mobilizing lymph and also as a direct means of treating skin cancers.

In neurological conditions this spice complex is highly beneficial, largely because of the infection connection to these syndromes. In this regard it must be the lead therapy for all chronic neurological conditions. As well, wild oregano therapy boosts the internal synthesis of protective enzymes within the neurons, notably superoxide dismutase, glutathione peroxidase, and catalase. Furthermore, for best results it is most ideal to consume not only the oil but also its associated supplements, the whole, crude herb complex, along with the aromatic essence. The aromatic essence and whole, crude herb contain compounds and biological complexes not found in the oil.

Let us also not forget its powers versus allergies, including acute reactions that are worrisome, the types that could lead to hospitalization and/or fatality. With the edible, daily use type, such worries, in some cases, horrors, are eliminated. Wild oregano oil is the most potent anti-allergy and antihistaminic agent known. Here, it is an absolute life- saver, quickly shutting down even the most toxic allergy reaction conceivable, like anaphylactic shock. Then, too, it is the optimal therapeutic agent for the typical allergic disorders, like hay fever, allergic rhinitis, hives, and food intolerance, all of which it routinely eliminates. This is true not only of the oil but also the aromatic essence as well as the whole, crude herbal complex.

Too, superior results are seen when associated biological factors are consumed, in particular, those which dramatically bolster the immune response, while also easing inflammation. These synergistic factors include unprocessed, whole food vitamin C complex, whole food, non-GM vitamin E, along with natural, whole food vitamins A and D. This is achieved either by consuming the whole

food, non-synthetic biological vitamin packet, at least one packet daily, and/or to take those vitamins separately. A reasonable protocol for overall health and immune system protection is as follows:

- oil of wild oregano
- whole, crude herb with *Rhus coriaria*
- juice or essence of wild oregano
- whole food vitamin C complex with wild camu camu, acerola, and rose hips

- whole food vitamin A and D complex from wild cod or sockeye salmon oil
- whole food, non-synthetic vitamin packet with
- unprocessed, food-source B complex, vitamin C, vitamin E, and vitamins A & D

Of note, vitamin A is highly synergistic with wild oregano. With a similar ORAC at 2800 per gram it also acts to block reactive cellular oxidation. Moreover, taken with this vitamin the oil prevents its oxidation, making this vitamin more potent in its actions, that is more biologically active. Once again, the vitamin A must be from non-synthetic sources, like whole food fish oil complexes, the types found in wild sockeye salmon oil, remote-source white fish oil, and natural, whole food burbot oil. Additionally, food sources of these fat-soluble vitamins should be consumed, including wild-source fatty fish, egg yolks, organic or pasture-fed butter, whole milk products, and fish roe.

So, for optimal health take the wild oregano, at least as the oil and, ideally, in its multiplicity of forms. For prevention consume it on a daily basis. It will bolster overall functions, including optimization of the health of the immune system, digestive system, while also bolstering cardiovascular and renal health. Rub the oil topically, as indicated. Use it on children and pets, as needed. Give it to children as a daily preventive. Remember, as long as it is from a whole food, wild, Mediterranean source it is safe for regular consumption. Take advantage of this immense blessing for better health and for the sake of preventing countless ailments. Think of it as a protection kit, a way to avoid health challenges to every degree. Take advantage of it, too, for combating that litany of chronic conditions for which it is highly effective, and which cause much suffering, including those syndromes deemed incurable.

The whole world must know about this. There is so much endless suffering that could be relieved through wild oregano therapy. It merely takes knowledge to comprehend this, which is thoroughly provided by this book. This is a proof of the truth of the old dictum, "Knowledge will set you free," in this case, freedom from disease.

Its uniqueness has been thoroughly described, how it simultaneously acts in a multiplicity of functions: as an antiseptic, antioxidant, anti-inflammatory agent, anti-pain agent, anti-toxin, and antihistamine. There is another novelty, which is the newly available and rather rare ultra- wild oregano oil formula with naturally occurring 84%-plus carvacrol. Highly penetrating and anti-inflammatory this is the ideal type for use in chronic or acute pain. It has been emphasized, too, how powerful it is for prevention. In this regard wild oregano can be consumed daily in reasonable amounts, that is the original, whole food, edible type, 100% wild, high-mountain source. Moreover, why not take advantage of it? This is in order to make life better and

easier, for the individual but also the entire family as well. No doubt, wild oregano will prevent great catastrophes, like the onset of dangerous, deadly diseases as well as unnecessary premature death. It is the obliterator of epidemics, the remedy of choice for all communicable diseases. For those who wish to avoid vaccinations it is the most essential therapeutic intervention to use. Wild oregano oil will save countless lives simply by taking it both preventively and also at the onset of infection, including the drug resistant types that kill in hospitals. People die unnecessarily. Edible, truly wild oregano oil fully prevents this. Nothing could be more profound than this. This is the degree of blessing that it alone can offer. No wonder the Prophet David praised it so highly, saying the body would be cleansed by it—of all deadly germs. Moreover, no wonder its users rave about it, because as they well know, without it, life would be far more difficult.

So, let us make life far easier and more pleasant than could possibly be conceived. Let us be free of all fear and worry, especially of infections. It is all through taking advantage of the greatest blessing of all—the divinely ordained wild oregano, its oil, the novel, newly available high-carvacrol ultra-potent formula, the aromatic essence, and the whole, crude wild herb: all powerful natural medicines, in fact, the most potent of all natural therapeutics known.

Chapter Fourteen

Appendix

Supplements Mentioned in This Book

The various supplements described in this book are listed in this appendix. However, it will be noted that they are mentioned generically. Here, the highest quality, most dependable wild oregano supplements are of Mediterranean origin, in the ancient lands now known as Turkey, Lebanon, and Syria. I mention this in order to guide people to make sound decisions, that is so people can purchase the most effective supplements available.

It can be seen through the following that the number of mentioned supplements is readily small and could be easily managed by those seeking to follow the given protocols. Truly whole food wild oregano oil is produced under the strictest degree of quality control. The same is true of whole food, crude herbal complex with *Rhus coriaria* as well as the juice or essence of wild oregano. Each batch is tested for levels of key active ingredients and has the full profile of not only potent phenolic compounds but also biologically active antioxidative terpenes. Individuals should consult their local health food stores to ensure that they are getting supplements that are authentic and effective. People can contact us at contact@purelywildnatural.com for a list of health food stores in their area. This is so the individual can take advantage of actual wild, medicinal plants and other therapeutic complexes for both the treatment of various conditions as well as disease prevention. After all, the various wild plants and their extracts are true gifts from God, made for human use as well as for the benefit of all other creation. So, take advantage of these natural complexes: for better health.

Chapter Fifteen

Bibliography

The Alternative Daily. 2013. This herb has 42x more antioxidants than apples. Oct. 15.

Afroditi, S., et al. 1996. Antimicrobial and cytotoxic activities of *origanum* essential oils. *J. Agric. Food Chem.* 44:1202.

Baser, K.H. 2008. Biological and pharmacological activities of carvacrol and carvacrol bearing essential oils. *Curr. Pharm. Des.* 143:3106.

Bendini, A., et al. 2002. Antioxidant activity of oregano leaves. *Ital. J. Food Sci.* 14:17.

Fan, K., Li, C., Cao, Y., Qi, H., Li, H., Zhang, Qu. and H. Sun. 2015. Carvacrol inhibits proliferation and induces apoptosis in human colon cancer cells. *Anticancer Drugs*. 26(8):813-2

Freidman, M. 2014.Chemistry and multibeneficial bioactivities of carvacrol (4-isopropyl-2-methylphenol), a component of essential oils produced by aromatic plants and spices. *J. Agric. Food Chem.* 6:7652-70.

Gilling, D. H., Kitajima, M., Torrey, J.R. and K. R. Bright. 2014. Antiviral efficacy and mechanisms of action of oregano essential oil and its primary component carvacrol against murine norovirus. *J Appl Microbiol.* 116(5):1149-63.

Ijaz, M.K., Ingram, C., et al. 2004. Antivral and viricidal activities of Oregano-based spice extracts against human coronavirus in-vitro. *Antiviral Research.* 62:121.

Ingram, C. 2005. *Natural Cures for Headaches.* Buffalo Grove, IL: Knowledge House Publishers.

Ingram, C. 2017. *The Cure is in the Cupboard.* Lake Forest, IL: Knowledge House Publishers.

Karaman, M., et al. 2017. Origanum vulgare essential oil affects pathogens causing vaginal infections. *J. Appl Microbiol.* 122:1177.

Manohar. V., Ingram, C., Gray, J., Talpur, N.A., Echard, B.W., Badchi, D., and H. G. Preuss. 2001. Antifungal activities of origanum oil against *Candida albicans. Mol Cell Biochem.* 228:111-7.

Marlete, B.C., et al. 2010. In vitro activity of origanum vulgare essential oil against candida species *Braz. J. Microbiol.* 41:116-123.

Preuss, H.G., et al. 2005. Effects of Essential Oils and Monolaurin on Staphylococcus aureus: In Vitro and In Vivo Studies. *Toxicol Mech Methods.* 2005;1:279-85

Science News, Oregano oil may protect against drug-resistant bacteria, Georgetown Researcher Finds. Oct. 11, 2001. Georgetown University Medical Center.

Uyanoglu, M., et al. 2008. Effects of carvacrol upon the liver of rats undergoing partial hepatectomy. *Phytomedicine.* 15:226-229.

Index

Index

About the Author

Cass Ingram is a nutritional physician who received a B.S. in biology and chemistry from the University of Northern Iowa (1979) and a D.O. from Des Moines Osteopathic College (1984). In the 1980's he started the Arlington Preventive Medical Center in Arlington Heights Illinois, which later became the American Center for Curative Medicine. Ingram was a pioneer in the holistic and preventive medical field. In the early nineties he stumbled upon wild oregano on a trip to his mother's home country of Lebanon, and after extensive research, he wrote the book *The Cure is in the Cupboard*. In fact, he has written 4 books and countless articles about oregano for medicinal purposes. He has written more than 25 books on natural healing and has given answers and hope to millions through interviews on thousands of radio and TV shows, as well as on his podcast *The Wilderness Doc*. His research and writing have led to countless nature based cures and discoveries. Cass Ingram presents hundreds of health tips and insights in his many books on health, nutrition, and disease prevention. He promotes the curative properties of wild medicinal foods and spice extracts. For more information see www.purelywildnatural.com.

Printed in Great Britain
by Amazon

39295273R00086